Academic Encounters

2nd Edition

Jennifer Wharton

Series Editor: Bernard Seal

READING
———
WRITING

CAMBRIDGE
UNIVERSITY PRESS

CAMBRIDGE UNIVERSITY PRESS
Cambridge, New York, Melbourne, Madrid, Cape Town,
Singapore, São Paulo, Delhi, Mexico City

Cambridge University Press
32 Avenue of the Americas, New York, NY 10013-2473, USA

www.cambridge.org
Information on this title: www.cambridge.org/9781107694507

First published 1999
Second edition 2013

Printed in the United States of America

A catalog record for this publication is available from the British Library.

ISBN 978-1-107-68363-1 Student's Book
ISBN 978-1-107-69450-7 Teacher's Manual

Additional resources for this publication at www.cambridge.org/academicencounters

Cambridge University Press has no responsibility for the persistence or
accuracy of URLs for external or third-party Internet Web sites referred to in
this publication and does not guarantee that any content on such Web sites is,
or will remain, accurate or appropriate. Information regarding prices, travel
timetables, and other factual information given in this work is correct at
the time of first printing but Cambridge University Press does not guarantee
the accuracy of such information thereafter.

Layout services: NETS, Bloomfield, CT

Table of Contents

Scope & Sequence   4

Introduction   8

Student Book Answer Keys   16

Content Quizzes   53

Content Quiz Answer Keys   61

Scope and Sequence

Unit 1: Planet Earth • 1

	Content	**R** Reading Skills	**W** Writing Skills
Chapter 1 The Physical Earth page 4	**Reading 1** Our Solar System **Reading 2** Earth's Four Systems **Reading 3** Rocks on Our Planet	Thinking about the topic Previewing art Asking and answering questions about a text Previewing key parts of a text	Parts of speech Comparative adjectives
Chapter 2 The Dynamic Earth page 27	**Reading 1** Plate Tectonics **Reading 2** Volcanoes **Reading 3** Earthquakes	Using headings to remember main ideas Building background knowledge about the topic Reading boxed texts Illustrating main ideas Thinking about the topic Reading for main ideas	Writing simple and compound sentences Writing definitions Pronoun reference Showing contrast

Unit 2: Water on Earth • 51

	Content	**R** Reading Skills	**W** Writing Skills
Chapter 3 Earth's Water Supply page 54	**Reading 1** The Water Cycle **Reading 2** Groundwater and Surface Water **Reading 3** Glaciers	Thinking about the topic Examining graphics Sequencing Reading about statistics Increasing reading speed Reading for main ideas Scanning	Identifying topic sentences Identifying topic sentences and supporting sentences Writing topic sentences and supporting sentences
Chapter 4 Earth's Oceans page 77	**Reading 1** Oceans **Reading 2** Currents **Reading 3** Waves and Tsunamis	Thinking about the topic Building background knowledge about the topic Reading maps Examining graphics Brainstorming Reading for main ideas and details	Writing about superlatives Describing results Concluding sentences Parallel structure *Both ... and* and *neither ... nor* Reviewing paragraph structure

V Vocabulary Skills	A Academic Success Skills	Learning Outcomes
Words from Latin and Greek Cues for finding word meaning Learning verbs with their prepositions	Highlighting Making a pie chart Answering multiple-choice questions Labeling diagrams	Write an academic paragraph about a place on Earth you like
Previewing key words Prefixes Prepositional phrases Using grammar, context, and background knowledge to guess meaning	Reading maps Answering true/false questions	

V Vocabulary Skills	A Academic Success Skills	Learning Outcomes
Antonyms Suffixes that change verbs into nouns Countable and uncountable nouns Subject-verb agreement	Understanding test questions Answering multiple-choice questions Mapping Conducting a survey	Write an academic paragraph about a water feature on earth
Subject-verb agreement *Too* and *very* Adjective suffixes	Taking notes Highlighting Labeling a map Organizing ideas	

Unit 3: The Air Around Us • 101

	Content	Ⓡ Reading Skills	Ⓦ Writing Skills
Chapter 5 **Earth's** **Atmosphere** page 104	**Reading 1** The Composition of the Atmosphere **Reading 2** The Structure of the Atmosphere **Reading 3** Clouds	Previewing key terms Building background knowledge about the topic Thinking about the topic Previewing key parts of a text Examining graphics Previewing art	Reviewing paragraph structure Transition words Writing about height Writing an observation report
Chapter 6 **Weather** **and Climate** page 127	**Reading 1** Climates Around the World **Reading 2** Storms **Reading 3** Hurricanes	Thinking about the topic Applying what you have read Previewing key parts of a text Increasing reading speed Reading for main ideas	Introducing examples

Unit 4: Life on Earth • 151

	Content	Ⓡ Reading Skills	Ⓦ Writing Skills
Chapter 7 **Plants and** **Animals** page 154	**Reading 1** Living Things **Reading 2** Plant Life **Reading 3** Animal Life	Thinking about the topic Building background knowledge about the topic Previewing key parts of a text	Writing about similarities Writing about differences Writing about similarities and differences
Chapter 8 **Humans** page 179	**Reading 1** The Brain **Reading 2** The Skeletal and Muscular Systems **Reading 3** The Heart and the Circulatory System	Thinking about the topic Applying what you have read Increasing reading speed Asking and answering questions about a text Scanning for details Building background knowledge about the topic Sequencing	Writing a description Writing about the body

V Vocabulary Skills	**A** Academic Success Skills	Learning Outcomes
Guessing meaning from context Describing parts Playing with words Colons, *such as*, and lists Words from Latin and Greek *When* clauses	Examining test questions Taking notes with a chart Using symbols and abbreviations	Write an academic paragraph about the climate in a place you know
Defining key words Using a dictionary Using *this/that/these/those* to connect ideas Synonyms Prepositions of location	Understanding averages Using a Venn diagram to organize ideas from a text Examining statistics Thinking critically about the topic	

V Vocabulary Skills	**A** Academic Success Skills	Learning Outcomes
Word families Defining key words Cues for finding word meaning *That* clauses Compound words	Answering true/false questions Asking for clarification Conducting a survey Making an outline Applying what you have read Thinking critically about the topic	Write an academic paragraph about the human body
Using adjectives Gerunds Words that can be used as nouns or verbs Prepositions of direction Playing with words	Highlighting and taking notes Using a dictionary Conducting an experiment Answering multiple-choice questions Highlighting and making an outline	

Introduction

The *Academic Encounters* Series

Academic Encounters is a sustained content-based series for English language learners preparing to study college-level subject matter in English. The goal of the series is to expose students to the types of texts and tasks that they will encounter in their academic course work and provide them with the skills to be successful when that encounter occurs.

At each level in the series, there are two thematically paired books. One is an academic reading and writing skills book, in which students encounter readings that are based on authentic academic texts. In this book, students are given the skills to understand texts and respond to them in writing. The reading and writing book is paired with an academic listening and speaking skills book, in which students encounter discussion and lecture material specially prepared by experts in their field. In this book, students learn how to take notes from a lecture, participate in discussions, and prepare short presentations.

The books at each level may be used as stand-alone reading and writing books or listening and speaking books. Or they may be used together to create a complete four-skills course. This is made possible because the content of each book at each level is very closely related. Each unit and chapter, for example, has the same title and deals with similar content, so that teachers can easily focus on different skills, but the same content, as they toggle from one book to the other. Additionally, if the books are taught together, when students are presented with the culminating unit writing or speaking assignment, they will have a rich and varied supply of reading and lecture material to draw on.

A sustained content-based approach

The *Academic Encounters* series adopts a sustained content-based approach, which means that at each level in the series students study subject matter from one or two related academic content areas. There are two major advantages gained by students who study with materials that adopt this approach.

- Because all the subject matter in each book is related to a particular academic discipline, concepts and language tend to recur. This has a major facilitating effect. As students progress through the course, what at first seemed challenging feels more and more accessible. Students thus gain confidence and begin to feel that academic study in English is not as overwhelming a task as they might at first have thought.

- The second major advantage in studying in a sustained content-based approach is that students actually gain some in-depth knowledge of a particular subject area. In other content-based series, in which units go from one academic discipline to another, students' knowledge of any one subject area is inevitably superficial. However, after studying a level of *Academic Encounters* students may feel that they have sufficiently good grounding in the subject area that they may decide to move on to study the academic subject area in a mainstream class, perhaps fulfilling one of their general education requirements.

The four levels in the series

The *Academic Encounters* series consists of four pairs of books designed for four levels of student proficiency. Each pair of books focuses on one or more related academic subject areas commonly taught in college-level courses.

- *Academic Encounters* 1: The Natural World
  Level 1 in the series focuses on earth science and biology. The books are designed for students at the low-intermediate level.

- *Academic Encounters* 2: American Studies
  Level 2 in the series focuses on American history, politics, government, and culture. The books are designed for students at the intermediate level.
- *Academic Encounters* 3: Life in Society
  Level 3 in the series focuses on sociological topics. The books are designed for students at the high-intermediate level.
- *Academic Encounters* 4: Human Behavior
  Level 4 in the series focuses on psychology and human communication. The books are designed for students at the low-advanced to advanced level.

New in the Second Edition

The second edition of the *Academic Encounters* series retains the major hallmark of the series: the sustained content approach with closely related pairs of books at each level. However, lessons learned over the years in which *Academic Encounters* has been on the market have been heeded in the publication of this brand new edition. As a result, the second edition marks many notable improvements that will make the series even more attractive to the teacher who wants to fully prepare his or her students to undertake academic studies in English.

New in the series

Four units, eight chapters per level. The number of units and chapters in each level has been reduced from five units / ten chapters in the first edition to four units / eight chapters in the second edition. This reduction in source material will enable instructors to more easily cover the material in each book.

Increased scaffolding. While the amount of reading and listening material that students have to engage with has been reduced, there has been an increase in the number of tasks that help students access the source material, including a greater number of tasks that focus on the linguistic features of the source material.

Academic Vocabulary. In both the reading and writing and the listening and speaking books, there are tasks that now draw students' attention to the academic vocabulary that is embedded in the readings and lectures, including a focus on the Academic Word list (AWL). All the AWL words encountered during the readings and lectures are also listed in an appendix at the back of each book.

Full color new design. A number of features have been added to the design, not only to make the series more attractive, but more importantly to make the material easier to navigate. Each task is coded so that teachers and students can see at a glance what skill is being developed. In addition, the end-of-unit writing skill and speaking skill sections are set off in colored pages that make them easy to find.

New in the reading and writing books

More writing skill development. In the first edition of *Academic Encounters*, the reading and writing books focused primarily on reading skills. In the second edition, the two skills are much more evenly weighted, making these books truly reading and writing books.

End-of-chapter and unit writing assignments. At the end of each chapter and unit, students are taught about aspects of academic writing and given writing assignments. Step-by step scaffolding is provided in these sections to ensure that students draw on the content, skills, and language they studied in the unit; and can successfully complete the assignments.

New and updated readings. Because many of the readings in the series are drawn from actual discipline-specific academic textbooks, recent editions of those textbooks have been used to update and replace readings.

New in the listening and speaking books

More speaking skill development. In the first edition of *Academic Encounters*, the listening and speaking books focused primarily on listening skills. In the second edition, the two skills in each of the books are more evenly weighted.

End-of-unit assignments. Each unit concludes with a review of the academic vocabulary introduced in the unit, a topic review designed to elicit the new vocabulary, and an oral presentation related to the unit topics, which includes step-by-step guidelines in researching, preparing, and giving different types of oral presentations.

New and updated lectures and interviews. Because the material presented in the interviews and lectures often deals with current issues, some material has been updated or replaced to keep it interesting and relevant for today's students.

Video of the lectures. In addition to audio CDs that contain all the listening material in the listening and speaking books, the series now contains video material showing the lectures being delivered. These lectures are on DVD and are packaged in the back of the Student Books.

The *Academic Encounters* Reading and Writing Books

Skills

There are two main goals of the *Academic Encounters* reading and writing books. The first is to give students the skills and confidence to approach an academic text, read it efficiently and critically, and take notes that extract the main ideas and key details. The second is to enable students to display the knowledge that has been gained from the reading either in a writing assignment or in a test-taking situation.

To this end, tasks in the *Academic Encounters* reading and writing books are color-coded and labeled as R 🅡 *Reading Skill* tasks, V 🅥 *Vocabulary Skill* tasks, W 🅦 *Writing Skill* tasks, and A 🅐 *Academic Success* tasks. At the beginning of each unit, all the skills taught in the unit are listed in a chart for easy reference.

- **Reading Skills 🅡.** The reading skill tasks are designed to help students develop strategies before reading, while reading, and after reading. The pre-reading tasks, such as Skimming for Main Ideas, teach students strategies they can employ to facilitate their first reading of a text. Post-reading tasks, such as *Identifying Main Ideas* and *Reading Critically* give students the tools to gain the deepest understanding possible of the text.

- **Vocabulary Skills 🅥.** Vocabulary learning is an essential part of improving one's ability to read an academic text. Many tasks throughout the books focus on particular sets of vocabulary that are important for reading in a particular subject area as well as the sub-technical vocabulary that is important for reading in any academic discipline. At the end of each chapter, some of the AWL words that appeared in the readings of the chapter are listed and an exercise is given that checks students' knowledge of those words.

- **Writing Skills 🅦.** There are two types of writing skills throughout the books. One type might more accurately be described as reading-for-writing skills in that students are asked to notice features of the texts that they have been reading in order to gain insight into how writers construct text. The other type is writing development skills, and these appear in the mid-unit and end-of-unit writing sections and overtly instruct students how to write academic texts, in which main ideas are supported with examples and in which plagiarism is avoided.

- **Academic Success 🅐.** Besides learning how to read, write, and build their language proficiency, students also have to learn other skills that are particularly important in academic settings. These include such skills as learning how to prepare for a content test, answer certain types of test questions, take notes, and work in study groups. *Academic Encounters* makes sure that this important dimension of being a student in which English is the medium of instruction is not ignored.

Readings

There are three readings in each chapter of the *Academic Encounters* reading and writing books. Readings vary in length and difficulty depending on the level of the book. The readings in the upper two levels contain texts that in many cases are unchanged from the college textbooks from which they were taken. The readings in the two lower-level books make use of authentic source materials. They are adapted so that they can be better processed by lower-level students, but great pains have been taken to retain the authentic flavor of the original materials.

Tasks

Before and after each reading, students are given tasks that activate one or more of the target skills in the book. The first time a task is introduced in the book, it is accompanied by a colored commentary box that explains which skill is being practiced and why it is important. When the task type occurs again later in the book, it is sometimes accompanied by another commentary box, as a reminder or to present new information about the skill. At the back of the book, there is an alphabetized index of all the skills covered in the tasks.

Order of units

In each book, a rationale exists for the order of the unit topics. Teachers may choose a different order if they wish; however, because reading skills and writing skills are developed sequentially throughout the books, teaching the units in the order that they occur is optimal. If teachers do choose to teach the units out of order, they can refer to the Skills Index at the back of the book to see what types of tasks have been presented in earlier units and build information from those tasks into their lessons.

Course length

Each unit in the *Academic Encounters* reading and writing books will take approximately 20 hours to teach. The six readings per unit should take about two to two and a half hours to teach, with about twenty minutes to be spent on the pre-reading activities. The two academic writing development sections can be taught as two writing workshops, each taking roughly two to two and a half hours to teach.

The course can be made shorter or longer. To shorten the course, teachers might choose not to do every task in the book and to assign some tasks and texts as homework, rather than do them in class. To lengthen the course, teachers might choose to supplement the book with content-related material from their own files, to assign Internet research, and to spend more time on the writing assignments.

Unit Content Quizzes

The *Academic Encounters* series adopts a sustained content-based approach in which students experience what it is like to study an academic discipline in an English-medium instruction environment. In such classes, students are held accountable for learning the content of the course by the administering of tests.

In the *Academic Encounters* series, we also believe that students should go back and study the content of the book and prepare for a test. This review of the material in the books simulates the college learning experience, and makes students review the language and content that they have studied.

At the back of this *Teacher's Manual* are four reproducible content quizzes, one for each unit in the book. Each quiz contains a mixture of true/false questions, multiple choice, and short-answer questions. The tests should take about 50 minutes of class time. Students should be given time to prepare for the test, but should take it as soon as possible after completing the unit.

General Teaching Guidelines

In this section, we give some very general instructions for teaching the following elements that occur in each unit of the *Academic Encounters* listening and speaking books:

- The unit opener, which contains a preview of the unit content, skills, and learning outcomes
- The *Preparing to Read* sections, which occur before each reading
- The *Readings*, which are sometimes accompanied by short boxed readings
- The *After You Read* sections, which follow each reading
- The *Academic Vocabulary Review* sections, which are at the end of each chapter
- The *Developing Writing Skills* sections, which are at the end of the first chapter of each unit
- The *Practicing Academic Writing* sections, which occur at the end of the second chapter of each unit

Unit Opener

The opening page of the unit contains the title of the unit, a photograph that is suggestive of the content of the unit, and a brief paragraph that summarizes the unit. Make sure that students understand what the title means. Have them look at the art on the page and describe it and talk about how it might relate to the title.

Finally look at the summary paragraph at the bottom of the page. Read it with your students and check to be sure that they understand the vocabulary and key concepts. At this point it is not necessary to introduce the unit topics in any depth, since they will get a detailed preview of the contents of the unit on the third page of the unit.

On the second page of the unit, students can preview the chapter and reading titles and see what skills are being taught throughout the unit. Have students read and understand the chapter and reading titles, and then focus on a few of the skills listed. Note those that students might already be familiar with and some new ones that are being taught for the first time in the book. Draw students' attention to the *Learning Outcomes* at the bottom of the page. This alerts students to what they are expected to be able to do by the end of the unit. It is also essentially a preview of the major assignment of the unit.

On the third page of the unit are tasks that preview the unit either by having students predict what information they might find in each section of the unit or by giving them some information from the unit and having them respond to it. The first couple of times that you teach from this page, tell students that when they are given a longer reading assignment, such as a chapter of a textbook, it is always a good strategy for them to preview the titles and headings of the reading, predict what the reading might be about, and to think about what they might already know about the subject matter.

The unit opener section should take about an hour of class time.

Preparing to Read

Each reading is preceded by a page of pre-reading tasks in a section called Preparing to Read. Pre-reading is heavily emphasized in the *Academic Encounters* reading and writing books since it is regarded as a crucial step in the reading process. Some pre-reading activities introduce students to new vocabulary; some teach students to get an overall idea of the content by surveying the text for headings, graphic material, captions, and art, and others have students recall their prior knowledge of the topic and their personal experiences to help them assimilate the material that they are about to encounter in the reading.

Although one or two pre-reading tasks are always included for each text, you should look for ways to supplement these tasks with additional pre-reading activities. As you and your students work your way through the book, students will become exposed to more and more pre-reading strategies. Having been exposed to these, students should be adding them to their repertoire, and you should encourage their regular use. For example, after having practiced the skill of examining graphic material, previewing headings and subheadings, and skimming for main ideas, students should ideally carry out these operations every time they approach a new reading.

As a general principle, the lower the proficiency level of the students, the greater is the need to spend time on the pre-reading activities. The more pre-reading tasks students undertake, the easier it is for students to access the text when it comes time for them to do a close reading.

Each *Preparing to Read* page should take about thirty minutes of class time. Some may require more or less time.

Reading

Once it comes time for students to read the text, how closely should they do so at this point? Some students believe that after doing the *Preparing to Read* tasks, they should now read the text slowly and carefully. They will be particularly tempted to do so because the texts have been crafted to be intentionally challenging for them, since students need to be prepared to read challenging, authentic, un-simplified text in their academic studies. However, students should be discouraged from doing this. For one thing, it is a poor use of class time to have students poring silently over a text for 20 minutes or more. More importantly, it is vital that students train themselves to read quickly, tolerating some ambiguity and going for understanding the main ideas and overall text structure, rather than every word and detail.

To promote faster reading, the book includes one *Increasing Reading Speed* task in most of the units. In this task, students are encouraged to read the text as quickly as possible, using techniques that can help them read faster while retaining a fairly high level of comprehension. If students consistently apply these techniques, most texts will take between 3 and 7 minutes to read. Before students start reading any text, therefore, it is a good idea to give them a challenging time limit, which they should aim toward to complete their reading of the text.

An alternative to reading every text in class is to assign some of the longer texts as homework. When you do this, you should do the pre-reading tasks in class at the end of the lesson and start the next class by having students quickly skim the text again before moving on to the *After You Read* tasks.

After You Read

Sometimes, after students have completed reading the text, the first order of business is not to move on to the *After You Read* tasks, but to revisit the Preparing to Read tasks to check to see if students had the correct answers in a predicting or skimming activity.

The tasks in the *After You Read* section are varied. Some focus on the content of the reading, some on the linguistic features of the reading, such as the vocabulary and grammar, and some on the organization of the text. There are also tasks that teach study skills. No two *After You Read* sections are the same (in fact, no two *After You Read* tasks are quite the same) because the content, organization, and the language of the reading dictate the types of tasks that would be appropriate.

Teachers who are used to more conventional post-reading tasks may be surprised to find that the focus of the post-reading is not text comprehension. This is because the intention of every task in the *Academic Encounters* reading and writing books is to develop a skill, not to test comprehension.

The following are the main functions of the post-reading activities in the *Academic Encounters* reading and writing books:

- to have students read for main ideas and think critically about the text
- to ask students to think about the content of the text, find a personal connection to it, or apply new information learned from the text in some way
- to highlight some of the most salient language in the text, either vocabulary or grammatical structures, and have students use that language in some way
- to have students gain insight into the style and organization of the text and to use those insights to help them become more effective writers themselves
- to develop students' repertoire of study skills by teaching them, for example, how to highlight a text, take notes, and summarize
- to develop students' test-preparation skills by familiarizing them with certain question types and by asking them to assess what they would need to do if they were going to be tested on the text.

To make the course as lively as possible, student interaction has been built into most activities. Thus, although the books are primarily intended to build reading and writing skills, opportunities for speaking abound. Students discuss the content of the texts, they work collaboratively to solve task problems, they compare answers in pairs or small groups, and sometimes they engage in role-playing.

Academic Vocabulary Review

The final exercise of each chapter lists words from the Academic Word List that students encountered in the chapter readings. The first time that you do this exercise, discuss the meaning of "academic word." Tell students that it is a word that occurs frequently across all types of academic texts regardless of the academic subject matter. As such, these are words that deserve students' special attention. Encourage students to learn these words and point out that at the back of the book there is an appendix of words from the Academic Word List that occurred in the readings. Promote the value of learning words from this appendix during their study of the course.

Developing Writing Skills

The *Developing Writing Skills* section of the unit occurs in the middle of the unit between the two chapters. In this section, students learn about some aspect of the writing process, such as how to write topic sentences, how to organize a paragraph or an essay, how to summarize, and how to avoid plagiarism. In the *Academic Encounters* reading and writing books Levels 1-2, the focus is primarily on learning how to write paragraphs. In the higher two levels, 3-4, the focus is on longer pieces of text, including academic essays.

In the first part of the section, the particular sub-skill that is the focus of the section is presented in an information box with clear examples. In the second part of the section, students are given a number of discrete activities to practice these writing sub-skills. Many of the activities in this section are collaborative. Teachers might therefore want to set up a writing workshop-style classroom when working on these sections, putting the students to work in pairs or small groups and circulating among them, checking on their progress and giving individualized feedback.

Practicing Academic Writing

The two sections of the unit that are devoted entirely to writing instruction are both set off on lightly-colored pages so that teachers can easily locate them throughout the book. This enables teachers or students to use them as reference sections and come back to them frequently as they work their way through the book.

The second writing section, *Practicing Academic Writing*, occurs at the very end of the unit. In this section, students are given a writing assignment and guided through steps in the writing process to help them satisfactorily complete the assignment. The writing assignments draw from content from the unit, so students are asked to go back to the readings in order to complete the assignments. In addition, students are reminded of any linguistic features that were the focus of instruction in the unit and are prompted to attempt to use such language in their own writing.

The *Practicing Academic Writing* section is divided into three parts: Preparing to Write, Now Write, and After You Write. In these three parts, students do pre-writing work (Preparing to Write), write a first draft (Now Write), and revise and edit their work (After You Write).

The *Practicing Academic Writing* section may well stretch over two or more class periods, with teachers varying the amount of in-class and out-of-class time spent on writing. The Preparing to Write part should be done in class. Here the students are presented with the assignment and are given some pre-writing activities that will aid them in writing their first draft. The *Now Write* part should at least sometimes be done in class so that teachers can accurately assess the strength of a student's writing.

It is recommended that teachers go through the *After You Write* part of the section in a different class from the first two parts of this section, so that they have a chance to provide feedback on students' writing and students have a chance to digest and apply that feedback. Remind students that good writers almost always write and re-write their texts several times and that the more re-writing of their texts that they do, the better writers they will eventually become.

Chapter 1
The Physical Earth

Reading 1 – Our Solar System

Preparing to Read

1 Thinking about the topic Page 4

Sample answers:

1. clouds, birds, the sun, rain, snow, and airplanes
2. stars, planets, the moon, airplane lights, meteors (shooting stars), lightning, and fireworks
3. *Answers will vary.*

2 Previewing art Page 4
A

1. There are eight planets: Mercury, Venus, Earth, Mars, Jupiter, Saturn, Uranus, and Neptune.
2. They are different in size, composition, and location.
3. The arrow should be pointing to the third planet from the sun, on the left.
4. The sun is the center. It is not a planet; it is a star.

B

1. an astronomer, Clyde Tombaugh
2. a telescope
3. They help people see objects that are very far away. *Answers will vary.*

After You Read

1 Asking and answering questions about a text Page 7
A

1. eight
2. "travel in a circle around a larger object"
3. The sun is a star.
4. *Answers will vary.*
5. *Answers will vary.*

2 Words from Latin and Greek Page 7
A

terrestrial (Par. 2, 3, 4), solar (Par. 1, 2, 5), astronomers (Par. 1, 5, Boxed Text), astronomical (Boxed Text)

Note: Though the word *solid* also appears in the reading, it does not derive from the same root as *solar*.

B

Word part from Latin or Greek	Meaning	English example	Meaning
terr-	earth, land	terrestrial	relating to Earth
sol-	sun	solar	*relating to the sun*
astro-	star	astronomer	*a scientist who studies stars and planets*

3 Cues for finding word meaning Page 8
A

1. parentheses
2. *that is*
3. *or*
4. parentheses

B

Sample answers:

1. constellations: groups of stars that form imaginary pictures and have names
2. extrasolar: outside of our solar system
3. supernova: an extremely bright explosion of a star
4. galaxy: a group of stars, gas, and dust held together by gravity.

C

Sample answers:

2. Earth is part of a solar system, that is, a star and the planets that move around it.
3. Mercury (the planet closest to the sun) is a terrestrial planet.
4. Jupiter is a gas giant planet, or a planet made of gases, not solid rock.

4 Parts of speech Page 9

A

Our <u>home</u> in the <u>universe</u> <u>is</u> planet <u>Earth</u>. It <u>is</u> one of (eight) <u>planets</u> that <u>orbit</u>, or <u>circle</u>, the <u>sun</u>. The <u>sun</u> <u>is</u> a <u>star</u>, that <u>is</u>, a (giant) <u>ball</u> of hot <u>gases</u>. It <u>is</u> the <u>center</u> of our (solar) <u>system</u>. There <u>are</u> <u>billions</u> of other <u>stars</u> in the <u>sky</u>, but the <u>sun</u> <u>is</u> the <u>star</u> closest to <u>Earth</u>. Our (solar) <u>system</u> also <u>includes</u> <u>moons</u>, which <u>orbit</u> <u>planets</u>. The <u>moon</u> we <u>see</u> in the (night) <u>sky</u> <u>orbits</u> <u>Earth</u>.

B

      n. v.   adj.   n.   n.   v. adj.
Mars is an interesting planet. In some ways, it is similar
        n.   v.   n.   n.   v.   n.
to Earth. It has weather and seasons. It also has canyons
          n.   n. v.   adj.   n.
and mountains. However, Mars is a very different planet
        n.   v.   adj.   n.   v.
from Earth. It is much smaller than Earth, and it is much
 adj.   v.   n.   n.
colder. In addition, there are no people on Mars.

C

2. adjective
3. noun
4. noun
5. verb

D

Sample answers:

2. terrestrial
3. rings
4. moon
5. think/believe

5 Comparative adjectives Page 11

A

four: smaller, farther, colder, darker

B

1. darker   2. hotter   3. more solid   4. icier
5. smaller   6. bigger   7. stronger   8. rockier

C

2. colder than   3. hotter than   4. closer . . . than
5. rockier than   6. larger than

D

Sample answers:

1. Jupiter is bigger than Pluto.
2. Jupiter is hotter than Pluto.
3. Pluto is darker than Jupiter.
4. Pluto is smaller than Jupiter.

Reading 2 – Earth's Four Systems

Preparing to Read

Previewing key parts of a text Page 12

B

1. four
2. lithosphere, hydrosphere, atmosphere, biosphere

C

Name of the system	Key feature(s)
lithosphere	Earth's crust and the top layer of the mantle
hydrosphere	water
atmosphere	air
biosphere	living things

After You Read

1 Highlighting Page 15

A

Sample answers:

- lithosphere: hard surface of Earth (Par. 2)
- hydrosphere: all the water on Earth (Par. 3)
- atmosphere: the air surrounding Earth (Par. 4)
- biosphere: all the living things on Earth (Par. 5)

B

Sample answers:

- We humans are part of the biosphere, but we live on the lithosphere. (Par. 6)
- We depend on the atmosphere for air to breathe and on the hydrosphere for water to drink. (Par. 6)

2 Words from Latin and Greek Pages 15–16

A

1. c
2. a
3. d
4. b

B

1. circle   2. rocks   3. water
4. gases   5. living things

C

- *lithology, atmospherology*
- *-logy* means "the study of something"

3 Learning verbs with their prepositions Page 16

A

1. from   2. from   3. with
4. on   5. to

B

2. Sunscreen and sunglasses protect people from the sun's dangerous rays.
3. The temperature on Pluto ranges from –238°C to –228°C.
4. Polar bears depend on a cold environment.
5. Drinking clean water and breathing clean air contribute to good health.

4 Making a pie chart Page 17

B

Sample answers:

- Approximately 3 percent of water on Earth is freshwater.
- Approximately 97 percent of water on Earth is saltwater.

Reading 3 – Rocks on Our Planet

Preparing to Read

1 Thinking about the topic Page 18

1. Photographs:
    a. Easter Island statues in the South Pacific
    b. the Great Pyramids in Egypt
    c. Machu Picchu in Peru
2. They are all made of rock.
3. **Sample answers:** Stonehenge in England, the Taj Mahal in India, the Parthenon in Greece, the Great Wall of China, El Tajín in Mexico
4. **Sample answers:** for building, tools, sculpture, and in gardens
5. *Answers will vary.*

2 Previewing key parts of a text Page 18

B

1. three
2. igneous, sedimentary, metamorphic
3. the process by which one type of rock changes into another type of rock

After You Read

1 Answering multiple-choice questions Page 21

1. d   2. a   3. d   4. c   5. b   6. b

2 Labeling diagrams Page 22

A

Left, top to bottom: lava, magma
Right: igneous rock

B

Counterclockwise from top: magma, igneous rock, sediment, sedimentary rock, metamorphic rock

3 Cues for finding word meaning   Page 23

A

2.

Earth is a terrestrial planet, that is, <u>a planet with a rocky surface</u>. (Par. 1)

All rocks are made of minerals, or inorganic (<u>nonliving</u>) matter. (Par. 1)

This process is called metamorphosis, or <u>the process of changing one thing into another</u>. (Par. 5)

B

the process of changing one thing into another

C

<u>This layer of little rocks is called</u> sediment.

<u>This process is called</u> the rock cycle.

D

Sample answers:

- Sediment is a layer of little rocks.
- The rock cycle is the process by which any type of rock changes to another type of rock.

Chapter 1 Academic Vocabulary Review   Page 24

1. professional	6. complex
2. features	7. design
3. process	8. cycle
4. diverse	9. ranges
5. area	10. primary

Developing Writing Skills

Writing Complete Sentences   Page 26

B

<u>The atmosphere</u> <u>is</u> the air surrounding Earth. <u>It</u> <u>is</u> made up of gases. <u>The primary gas</u> <u>is</u> nitrogen. <u>The gases</u> in the atmosphere <u>create</u> air for us to breathe. <u>They</u> also <u>protect</u> Earth from the sun's ultraviolet radiation. <u>Clouds</u> <u>form</u> in the atmosphere. <u>These clouds</u> <u>produce</u> rain and snow.

C

Narenda Luther ~~having~~ ^{has} something very unusual in his house. ~~Is~~ ^{It is} a giant, two-billion-year-old stone.

This rock ^{is} just one of many in the city of Hyderabad, India. The people in the city ~~they~~ named some of the rocks. ~~Used~~ ^{They used} many to make temples or billboards.

People ~~destroying~~ ^{destroyed} other rocks to make room for new development.

Corrected paragraph:

Narenda Luther has something very unusual in his house. It is a giant, two-billion-year-old stone. This rock is just one of many in the city of Hyderabad, India. The people in the city named some of the rocks. They used many to make temples or billboards. People destroyed other rocks to make room for new development.

D

Sample answers:

- Earth is one of eight planets in our solar system.
- It orbits the sun, and it has one moon.
- It is larger than Pluto and smaller than Jupiter.
- Earth is a special place.
- It is the only planet in our solar system with life.
- Earth has four interconnected systems: the lithosphere, the hydrosphere, the atmosphere, and the biosphere.
- Earth has more water than land.
- There are many different types of living things on Earth.
- Earth is a rocky planet.
- The three types of rocks on Earth are igneous, sedimentary, and metamorphic.
- The rocks on Earth change form over time.

Chapter 2
The Dynamic Earth

Reading 1 – Plate Tectonics

Preparing to Read

Previewing key words Page 27
B

2. d   3. a   4. c   5. f   6. b

After You Read

1 Using headings to remember main ideas Page 30
B

1. b   2. c   3. a   4. d

2 Prefixes Page 31
B

1. interplanetary   2. century

3. convention   4. millennium

C

Sample answers:

cent-: cents, centigrade, centimeter, centipede
con-: conference, Congress, connect, contact,
            conversation
inter-: intercultural, interfere, intermission, international,
             interview
mil-: milligram, milliliter, millimeter, millipede

3 Prepositional phrases Page 31
A

2. Where?   3. When?   4. Where?
5. How?   6. How?

B

Sample answers:

- under the oceans (Where?)
- in different directions (How? / Where?)
- in Asia (Where?)
- between the Pacific Plate and the North American Plate (Where?)
- over a long period of time (When?)
- in dramatic ways (How?)

4 Reading Maps Page 32
B

1. T
2. F
3. F
4. T
5. T

5 Writing simple and compound sentences Page 32
A

Sample answers:

Simple sentences:

- <u>Earth</u> is always <u>moving</u>. (Par. 1)
- <u>A good example</u> is the Atlantic Ocean. (Par. 4)
- <u>This process</u> <u>created</u> the Himalayas, the great mountain range in Asia. (Par. 5)

Compound sentences:

- <u>You</u> <u>may not feel</u> it, (but) <u>our whole planet</u> <u>is turning</u> as <u>it</u> <u>orbits</u> the sun. (Par. 1)
- <u>He</u> <u>called</u> his idea continental drift theory, (but) <u>this idea</u> <u>did not explain</u> how the continents moved. (Par. 2)
- Today <u>the Atlantic</u> <u>is</u> a huge ocean, (and) <u>the Mid-Atlantic Ridge</u> <u>is</u> the longest mountain range on Earth. (Par. 4)

B

Sample answers:

- In continental drift theory, Pangaea was the name of Earth's one huge continent.
- Earth's crust is broken into many pieces, and these pieces are called tectonic plates.
- Tectonic plates are under the continents and under the oceans.
- At divergent boundaries, plates move away from each other.
- At convergent boundaries, plates move toward each other, and sometimes this movement forms mountains.

Reading 2 – Volcanoes

Preparing to Read

Building background knowledge about the topic Page 33

B

1. *Answers will vary.*
2. **Sample answers:** Mt. Vesuvius (Italy), Mt. Fuji (Japan), Mt. Tambora (Indonesia), Mt. Krakatau (Indonesia), Mt. Pelée (Martinique), Mt. St. Helens (Washington, U.S.A.), Mt. Kilauea (Hawaii, U.S.A.), Mt. Llullaillaco (Argentina-Chile), Mt. Etna (Italy), Mt. Pinatubo (Philippines).
3. *Answers will vary.*

C

1. b   2. d   3. a   4. c

After You Read

1 Answering true/false questions Page 36

A

1. T   2. F   3. T   4. T
5. F   6. F   7. T   8. F

B

1. Par. 2   2. Par. 2   3. Par. 2   4. Par. 3
5. Par. 3   6. Par. 4   7. Par. 4   8. Par. 6

C

Sample answers:

2. The Ring of Fire is around the Pacific Plate.
5. Many volcanic eruptions, over millions of years, formed the Hawaiian Islands.
6. Today the world has approximately 1,500 active volcanoes.
8. Volcanoes can have both positive and negative effects on Earth.

2 Writing definitions Page 37

A

Sample answers:

1. A hot spot is a hole in Earth's crust that magma flows through; the lava eventually forms a volcanic island.
2. An active volcano is a volcano that is erupting now or that could erupt in the future.

B

Sample answers:

1. Tectonic plates are large pieces of Earth's crust under the continents and the oceans.
2. A ridge is a chain/range of mountains.
3. An earthquake is a movement of Earth's crust.

3 Reading boxed texts Page 37

B

Sample answer:

Yes. It gives an interesting example of an idea in the main text.

C

Sample answers:

"The Story of Pluto": discusses a topic that is closely related to the topic of the main text.

"Save the Rocks!": gives an interesting example of an idea in the main text. It also discusses a topic that is closely related to the topic of the main text.

Reading 3 – Earthquakes

Preparing to Read

Thinking about the topic Page 39

A

Sample answers:

1. broken roads, damaged houses and buildings
2. an earthquake
3. *Answers will vary.*

B

Sample answers:

1. An earthquake is something that makes the ground shake.
2. Some places have more earthquakes because tectonic plates under those places move around a lot and bump into each other.
3. and 4. *Answers will vary.*
5. To stay safe, get away from things that can fall on you, get low to the ground, cover your head, and hold on to something.

After You Read

1 Reading for main ideas Page 42
A

1. Par. 3   2. Par. 1   3. Par. 2   4. Par. 4

B

2

2 Using grammar, context, and background knowledge to guess meaning Page 43

B

b. sensed   c. bark   d. collapsed   e. upset

3 Pronoun reference Page 44
A

2. the two plates (Par. 2)
3. a strong movement (Par. 2)
4. The deadliest earthquake (Par. 3)

4 Showing contrast Page 45
A

1. However   2. but   3. However   4. but

B

Sample answers:

2. California has earthquakes every day, but only a few of them are strong enough for people to feel.
   California has earthquakes every day. However, only a few of them are strong enough for people to feel.
3. Small earthquakes do not shake the ground very much, but large earthquakes can destroy buildings.
   Small earthquakes do not shake the ground very much. However, large earthquakes can destroy buildings.

4. You may not feel the ground move, but our planet moves all the time.
   You may not feel the ground move. However, our planet moves all the time.

Chapter 2 Academic Vocabulary Review

Page 46

1. region
2. create
3. Normally
4. theory
5. survive
6. accurate
7. predict
8. collapsed
9. interact
10. major

Practicing Academic Writing

Preparing to Write

1 Using correct paragraph form Pages 47–48
A

Sample answers:

The first sentence is indented. Each sentence begins with a capital letter, and each sentence ends with appropriate punctuation. Each sentence directly follows the sentence before it.

B

There are four basic types of volcanoes: shield volcanoes, composite volcanoes, cinder cone volcanoes, and supervolcanoes. Shield volcanoes are generally very large, and lava usually flows down their sides. Composite volcanoes are smaller than shield volcanoes. They can have both small eruptions and big eruptions. The smallest type of volcano is the cinder cone volcano. For example, the Paricutín volcano was a cinder cone volcano. The largest and most dangerous volcanoes are supervolcanoes, and they can cause a lot of destruction. Scientists continue to study the four types of volcanoes to learn more about our planet.

2 Using correct paragraph structure Pages 48–49

Earthquakes can happen anywhere, but certain places have more earthquakes. [These places sit on tectonic plates that move frequently. One example is the area around the Pacific Plate, which includes China, the Philippines, Japan, and the western coasts of Canada, the United States, and South America. Earthquakes are common in those places. The deadliest earthquake in modern times happened in 1976 in Tangshan, China. It lasted less than two minutes, but more than 250,000 people died, and more than 90 percent of the buildings collapsed.] Earthquake scientists study places such as Tangshan because of the many faults in these areas and the activity of the tectonic plates. (Par. 3)

TS

SS

CS

C

1. Yes.
2. There are eight supporting sentences.
3. Yes.

There is no way to stop an earthquake, but there are several things you can do to prepare and protect yourself. [Before an earthquake happens, you should make an emergency plan. You should also prepare an emergency supply kit with a battery-powered radio, a flashlight, and enough food and water for three days. Remember to do these things during an earthquake: Stay away from windows and tall furniture inside a building. Get on the floor, cover your head, and hold on to something until the shaking stops. Find a place away from buildings and trees outside and get on the ground. After the earthquake stops, check for injuries – are you hurt? Listen to the radio for instructions. If you are in an unsafe building, go outside.] An earthquake can be a frightening experience, but knowing what to do before, during, and after it will help you stay safe.

TS

SS

CS

Now Write

Sample paragraph:

The most beautiful place on Earth that I know is Denali National Park in Alaska. It is a great place to enjoy nature. There are green trees and colorful flowers everywhere, and you can hike for days. You can see bald eagles, bears, moose, and many other animals. They live happily and freely in the park. You can see all this natural beauty, but you do not see any pollution or trash. The air, water, and land are very clean. For all these reasons, Denali National Park is my favorite place.

Chapter 3
Earth's Water Supply

Previewing the Unit

Chapter 3: Earth's Water Supply Page 53
A

a. lake   b. river   c. glacier

Chapter 4: Earth's Oceans Page 53
B

1. d   2. c   3. e   4. b   5. a

Reading 1 – The Water Cycle

Preparing to Read

1 Thinking about the topic Page 54
A

Sample answers:

1. *Water* would be a good name for our planet because there is much more water than land.
2. Some places you can find water are lakes, rivers, ponds, streams, glaciers, oceans, seas, and under the ground.
3. The word *essential* means "very important; necessary, required." The word *decrease* means "to get smaller; to become less in amount."

B

1. and 2. *Answers will vary.*
3. **Sample answer:** The amount of water on Earth never decreases because the water cycle recycles the planet's water. For example, water in the ocean evaporates, forms clouds, rains, and then the water is returned to Earth into an ocean or river.

2 Examining graphics Page 54
A

Sample answer:
The word *cycle* means "a complete process" or "a complete set of steps."

B

Sample answer:
The water cycle is the process by which water moves from Earth into the atmosphere and back to Earth again.

After You Read

1 Understanding test questions Page 57
A

1. <u>How much</u> of <u>Earth</u> is covered by <u>water</u>? The question is asking for an amount/number. (more than 70 percent)
2. <u>How many steps</u> does the <u>water cycle</u> have? The question is asking for an amount/number. (three steps)
3. <u>Where</u> does <u>water evaporate</u> from? The question is asking for a place. (from anywhere there is water and sun, such as oceans, lakes, rivers)
4. <u>Why</u> does <u>water vapor change</u> back to <u>liquid water</u>? The question is asking for an explanation/reason. (because it rises into the atmosphere and cools)
5. <u>Where</u> is the <u>fastest water cycle</u> on Earth? The question is asking for a place. (in tropical rain forests)
6. <u>Why</u> is the <u>water on Earth</u> today actually <u>millions of years old</u>? The question is asking for an explanation/reason. (because the water cycle keeps recycling the same water over and over again)

B

Sample answers:

1. Why is the water cycle so slow in the desert? (because deserts are very dry and it doesn't rain often)
2. Where does the water go when it falls back to Earth as rain? (some of the water goes into the ground, and some goes into lakes, rivers, and oceans)

2 Sequencing Page 58
A

a. 3   b. 7   c. 8   d. 4
e. 6   f. 2   g. 1   h. 5

B

Diagrams will vary, but they all should include the steps shown in Figure 3.1 on Student's Book page 56.

3 Antonyms Page 59

A

1. d   2. e   3. f   4. a   5. c   6. b

B

Sample answers:

1. The temperature where I live heats up during the day, but it cools down at night.
   The temperature where I live heats up during the day. However, it cools down at night.
2. My sister is the slowest runner in our family, but she is the fastest talker.
   My sister is the slowest runner in our family. However, she is the fastest talker.
3. The pond near my house is small, but the lake in the park is large.
   The pond near my house is small. However, the lake in the park is large.

4 Suffixes that change verbs into nouns Pages 59–60

A

1. movement   2. evaporation   3. condensation
1. form   2. combine   3. continue

B

1. V assign   4. V evaporate
2. N eruption   5. N location
3. N information   6. V moves

5 Identifying topic sentences Page 60

A

Par. 2: Evaporation is the first step in the water cycle.
Par. 3: Condensation is the second step in the water cycle.
Par. 4: The third step in the water cycle is precipitation.

B

1. main idea: Plants found in tropical rain forests are important sources of food and medicine for humans.
2. c

Reading 2 – Groundwater and Surface Water

Preparing to Read

1 Thinking about the topic Page 61

1. saltwater
2. ice
3. **Sample answers:** wells, water tanks, the public water supply, bottled water
4. Most people have access to safe drinking water (approximately 80%).
5. *Answers will vary.*
6. **Sample answers:** water conservation, water recycling, desalination, water purification, digging more wells
7. *Answers will vary.* Some studies have shown that a healthy person at a normal weight can live for more than a month without food if they continue to drink water, but can only live about a week without water.

2 Examining graphics Page 61

1. saltwater
2. 97%
3. 20%
4. 79%
5. 1%

After You Read

1 Answering multiple-choice questions Page 64

A

1. d   2. b   3. a   4. c   5. d   6. c

2 Mapping Page 65

B

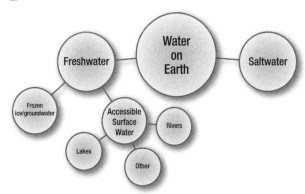

4 Countable and uncountable nouns Pages 66–67
A

Sample answers:

Countable nouns: liters, spaces, rocks, area(s), well, aquifer(s), cracks, lakes, rivers, gallons
Uncountable nouns: water, rain, snow, sand, saturation, groundwater, earth

B
1. C   2. U   3. U   4. C   5. C

5 Reading about statistics Page 67
A
1. agriculture   2. 3%   3. frozen   4. no

B
c (80 percent = four-fifths)   d (20 percent = one-fifth)
f (50 percent = one-half)   a (25 percent = one-fourth)
e (33 percent = one-third)   b (10 percent = one-tenth)

C
1. 80%   2. 1/5
3. Almost 50%   4. More than 1/4

Reading 3 – Glaciers
Preparing to Read
Increasing reading speed Page 68
C
1. c   2. a   3. b

After You Read
1 Reading for main ideas Page 71
A
1. Par. 4   2. Par. 2   3. Par. 5   4. Par. 1   5. Par. 3

B
3

2 Scanning Page 71
1. Alberta, Canada (Par. 1)
2. 41 meters (Par. 1)
3. 400 kilometers (Par. 1)
4. U-shaped (Par. 4)
5. Norway, Alaska, and Japan (Par. 4)
6. India (Boxed text)
7. 12 (Boxed text)

3 Subject-verb agreement Page 72
1. forms, turns
2. is
3. contain
4. has

4 Identifying topic sentences and supporting sentences Page 73
B
Glaciers change the surface of our planet in different ways.

C
One way is by shaping the land. Another way glaciers change Earth is by creating lakes.

D
For example, glaciers carve U-shaped valleys and form sharp mountaintops. Glaciers can also move big rocks to other locations. For instance, Mirror Lake and the Great Lakes in the United States were formed by glaciers. Lake Louise in Canada is another example.

F
1. T   2. T   3. F

5 Writing topic sentences and supporting sentences Page 73
A and B

Sample answers:

1. Topic sentence: Lakes are an important source of freshwater on Earth.
   Major support: There are many lakes on our planet.
   Minor support: In fact, there are millions of lakes that contain freshwater.
2. Topic sentence: Glaciers are very important to life on Earth.
   Major support: They are a major source of freshwater.
   Minor support: For example, glaciers contain more than 75 percent of Earth's freshwater.

Chapter 3 Academic Vocabulary Review

Page 74

1. percent
2. global
3. energy
4. generations
5. source
6. environment
7. accessible
8. occur
9. Environmentalists
10. contrast

Developing Writing Skills

Pages 75–76

B

(The first type of desert is the hot desert.) For instance, the Mojave and the Sahara are both hot deserts. <u>These deserts have high temperatures in the daytime, cooler temperatures at night, and just a little rain. Their average temperatures are 20°–25°C and most receive less than 15 centimeters of rain each year. Only a few plants, such as prickly pears and acacias, can live in hot deserts.</u> (The second type of desert is the cold desert.) The Gobi and Namib are both examples of cold deserts. <u>Some cold deserts have high temperatures in the summer, but very cold temperatures in the winter. The average winter temperatures are −2° to 4°C. Cold deserts have almost no rain, but some snow. On average, they receive 15–26 centimeters of snow each year. There are only a few plants, such as sagebrush, in cold deserts.</u> These differences clearly show that all deserts may be dry, but they are not all the same.

1. two
2. the first type, the second type
3. They explain the major supporting sentences; they also include examples, facts, and statistics.

C

Sample answer:
Earth has two very different types of deserts.

E

Set A

■ Check the faucets in your home for leaks, and fix any problems.
■ One leaky faucet can waste more than seven liters of water each day.
■ Try to take shorter showers.
■ For example, if you take a 5-minute shower instead of a 10-minute shower, you could save almost a 100 liters of water.

Set B

■ Many people believe that the Nile River is the longest river in the world.
■ It is more than 6,500 kilometers long and flows through nine countries, including Egypt, Kenya, and Tanzania.
■ The Yangtze River is the most famous river in China.
■ It is about 4,990 kilometers long and divides northern China and southern China.

F

Set A: Easy ways to save water at home
Set B: The Nile and the Yangtze are two of the world's most famous rivers.

G

Sample paragraph:
   Rivers and lakes affect our lives in many ways, both good and bad. One good way is by providing us with things we need to survive. For example, rivers and lakes give us freshwater and food. Another way rivers and lakes help us is by providing a place for outdoor sports. For instance, many people enjoy swimming, boating, and fishing. However, rivers and lakes also affect us in bad ways. For example, they often flood during heavy rains, and this can cause a lot of damage to nearby homes and businesses. In addition, sometimes the water in rivers and lakes is polluted, and we cannot use it. These are just a few of the ways that rivers and lakes influence our lives.

Chapter 4
Earth's Oceans

Reading 1 – Oceans

Preparing to Read

1 Thinking about the topic Page 77

Sample answers:

1. four (or five): Pacific Ocean, Atlantic Ocean, Indian Ocean, Arctic Ocean, (Southern or Antarctic Ocean)
2. Oceans are bigger than rivers and lakes; they have tides, waves, and currents.
3. Ocean water tastes salty.
4. Some living things in the ocean are fish, whales, sharks, coral, seaweed, dolphins, starfish, eels, and turtles.
5. Oceans are important because they are part of the water cycle, they influence climate, and they provide food, jobs, transportation routes, and recreation.
6. They worry about pollution and rising sea levels.

2 Building background knowledge about the topic Page 77

Sample answers:

1. So many people live near an ocean because oceans are a big part of Earth (70 percent).
2. Some advantages of living near oceans are that they are beautiful and relaxing to look at, they provide recreation, and they keep the climate from being too dry.
3. When many people live near an ocean, they may pollute it.
4. If the water level of the ocean rises, it will probably cause flooding. Some people might die, and others would have to move; this would make other places more crowded.

After You Read

1 Taking notes Page 80

Sample answers:

Oceans
General info
  5 oceans: Pacific, Atlantic, Indian, Arctic, Southern
  Cover more than 70% of Earth's surface (Par. 1)

Main oceans & features
  Pacific: largest, deepest, often violent
  Atlantic: 2nd largest, covers 1/5 of Earth's surface
  Indian: calmest, smaller than Atlantic (Par. 2, 3)
Salinity (= saltiness)
  Ocean water = 96.5% water + 3.5% salt
  Depends on: 1) amount of evaporation
              2) amount of freshwater
  Higher near the equator, lower near the poles & the places where large rivers empty into oceans (Par. 4)
Importance of oceans
  Ex: 1. Role in water cycle
      2. Provide food
      3. Provide jobs
      4. Home for many plants & animals
      5. People like to live nearby (Par. 6)

2 Reading maps Page 81
A

Light blue = less salinity
Medium blue = medium salinity
Dark blue = more salinity

B
1. L   2. L   3. H   4. M

3 Writing about superlatives
Pages 82–83
A
Seven: largest (Par. 2), deepest (Par. 2), second-largest (Par. 3), calmest (Par. 3), smallest (Par. 3), coldest (Par. 3), lowest (Par. 5)

B
1. largest
2. coldest
3. smallest
4. saltiest
5. most peaceful
6. most important

C
2. the most violent   3. the calmest
4. the smallest

4 Describing results Page 83
A

- Together, the oceans cover more than 70 percent of Earth's surface, and they flow into each other. <u>Therefore, from outer space it looks as if Earth has one huge blue ocean.</u> [Yes] (Par. 1)
- The first time that the explorer Ferdinand Magellan sailed on this huge ocean, it was a calm day. <u>That's why Magellen named the ocean *Mar Pacífico* – that is, "peaceful ocean" or "calm ocean" in Magellan's native language of Portuguese.</u> [Yes] (Par. 2)
- In cold areas near the North Pole and the South Pole, oceans are not as salty. There is less evaporation, and the oceans receive freshwater from melting glaciers. <u>Therefore, salinity is lower in polar areas.</u> [Yes] (Par. 5)
- The lowest salinity levels occur where large rivers empty into an ocean. <u>That's why the place where the giant Amazon River flows into the Atlantic Ocean is less salty than the rest of the ocean.</u> [Yes] (Par. 5)

B

1. b   2. a   3. d   4. c

1. The five oceans flow into each other. (Therefore, / That's why) from outer space, it looks as if Earth has one huge ocean.
2. When Magellan first sailed on the Pacific, it was calm. (Therefore, / That's why) he named the ocean Mar Pacífico, which means "peaceful ocean."
3. In areas near the equator, there is a lot of evaporation and not a lot of rain. (Therefore, / That's why) ocean water near the equator usually has higher levels of salinity.
4. Fresh river water dilutes the salt in ocean water. (Therefore, / That's why) the place where the Amazon River empties into the Atlantic Ocean is less salty than the rest of the ocean.

5 Concluding sentences Page 84
A
CS: Therefore, from outer space it looks as if Earth has one huge blue ocean. Compared to TS: One nickname for Earth is the "blue planet."

B
3

C
Sample answer:
Clearly, Jacques-Yves Cousteau made a great contribution to the world's oceans.

Reading 2 – Currents
Preparing to Read

1 Thinking about the topic Page 85
B
Sample answers:

1. the wind
2. the Gulf Stream, the Circumpolar Current, the Humboldt Current, and the California Current
3. They spread the heat from the sun around the Earth, they affect water temperature, and they can influence climate.
4. a strong current that travels very fast

2 Examining graphics Page 85
1. T   2. F   3. T   4. F
5. T   6. T   7. F   8. F

After You Read

1 Highlighting Page 88
A
Sample answers:

- Currents are rivers of water that flow through the ocean. (Par. 1, 2, 3, 4, Boxed text)
- The Gulf Stream is a huge warm-water current that starts in the Gulf of Mexico, and then flows along the east coast of North America to northern Europe. (Par. 3)
- Rip currents are small currents that are often dangerous because they flow quickly away from the shore and out into the ocean. (Boxed text)
- Trade winds are winds near the equator that blow from east to west. (Par. 2)
- Westerlies are winds that blow from west to east between the equator and the poles. (Par. 2)

B

Sample answers:

1. The main cause of surface currents is wind. (Par. 2)
2. In general, surface currents in the ocean follow a circular path. They travel west along the equator, turn as they reach a continent, travel east until they reach another area of land, and then go west along the equator again. (Par. 2)
3. Surface currents help spread the heat from the sun around Earth. (Par. 3)
4. They move water in big circles. This causes cold water to move to warmer places, and warm water to move to cooler places. It prevents, or stops, warm water near the equator from becoming too hot. It also prevents cold water near the North and South poles from becoming too cold.
   Currents affect the temperature of ocean water and the temperature on land. The moving water of currents heats or cools the air around them. (Par. 3)
5. . . . the Gulf Stream . . . . begins in the Gulf of Mexico, flows past the East Coast of North America, and eventually reaches northern Europe. (Par. 3)
6. Rip currents are small currents that flow away from the shore and out into the ocean . . . . dangerous because they travel very fast. . . . can carry a swimmer too far out into the ocean in less than a minute. (Boxed text)

2 Labeling a map Page 88
A

Compass labels should match those in Figure 4.1 on Student's Book page 86.

Labels on map:

1. North Pole
2. equator
3. South Pole
4. trade winds
5. the westerlies
6. Gulf Stream

3 Subject-verb agreement Page 89
A

1. is   2. flows   3. travel   4. are   5. have

B

1. There is a cold ocean current near the coast of California.
2. A warm current near the coast of Japan flows from south to north.
3. Currents by the equator generally travel in a westward direction.
4. There are winds called tropical trade winds near the equator.
5. Currents in the ocean have an effect on Earth's climates.

4 *Too* and *very* Page 89
A

- These currents are small, but they can be extremely dangerous because they travel <u>very</u> fast.
- A powerful rip current can carry a swimmer <u>too</u> far out into the ocean in less than a minute.
- The swimmer gets <u>very</u> nervous and tries to swim back to shore against the powerful current.
- The swimmer becomes <u>too</u> tired to swim anymore and then drowns.

B

1. too   2. very   3. very   4. too

Reading 3 – Waves and Tsunamis

Preparing to Read

1 Brainstorming Page 90

Sample answers:
Ways oceans influence people's lives:

- Oceans provide food and jobs.
- They influence climate.
- They play an important role in the water cycle.
- They provide transportation routes.
- They provide recreation.
- They can destroy homes and kill people when there is flooding, or when storms or tsunamis happen.

After You Read

1 Reading for main ideas and details   Page 93

1. M	2. D	3. D	4. M
5. D	6. D	7. M	8. D

2 Adjective suffixes   Pages 93–94
A

1. beautiful	2. enjoyable	3. predictable
4. dangerous	5. careful	6. powerful

B

1. enjoyable	2. dangerous	3. powerful
4. careful	5. predictable	6. beautiful

3 Parallel structure   Page 94
A

The ocean can be both beautiful and enjoyable. Many people like walking on the beach and watching the water. Others enjoy swimming, surfing, and sailing. However, the ocean is not predictable, and it can be very dangerous. Wind can create big waves that knock people down, sink boats, and damage the shoreline. Giant waves, called tsunamis, can kill people and wash away entire towns. The ocean is truly a place of great beauty and great danger.

B

1. The ocean can be beautiful and ~~enjoyment~~ enjoyable. (Par. 1)
2. Many people like walking on the beach and ~~to watch~~ watching the water. (Par. 1)
3. The wind can create big waves that knock people down, sink boats, and ~~damaged~~ damage the shoreline. (Par. 1)
4. The power of the ~~windy~~ wind and the waves can be deadly. (Par. 3)
5. The tsunamis killed more than 250,000 people and ~~destroying~~ destroyed hundreds of towns. (Par. 5)

4 Both . . . and and neither . . . nor   Page 95
A

Four sentences:

- The ocean can be both beautiful and enjoyable. (Par. 1)
- Most waves are neither very big nor dangerous. (Par. 3)
- Neither winds nor waves create tsunamis. (Par. 4)
- The next time you go to the beach, take a few moments to appreciate both the beauty and the danger of the ocean. (Par. 6)

B

1. waves
2. volcanoes
3. Southern
4. preventable
5. dangerous

5 Reviewing paragraph structure   Page 95

Sample answers:

Topic sentence: Duke Kahanamoku shared his love of surfing with the world, and he helped make surfing a popular sport in many countries.

Concluding sentence: That's why many people think Duke Kahanamoku was one of the most important surfers in history.

Chapter 4 Academic Vocabulary Review

Page 96

1. similar	6. jobs
2. varies	7. factors
3. widespread	8. approach
4. removed	9. affect
5. parallel	10. appreciate

Practicing Academic Writing

Preparing to Write

Choosing a topic, exploring ideas, and making a simple outline

Pages 97–98

A

1. b   2. d   3. d

After You Write

Writing on topic   Page 100

A

Ocean water is warm near the equator.

B

1. The California Current makes the climate of the Hawaiian Islands cooler than we might expect, too.
2. Peru and Ecuador are countries in South America.

E

Sample paragraph:

The Indian Ocean

The Indian Ocean is one of Earth's five oceans. It is located between Africa, Asia, Australia, and Antarctica. The Indian Ocean is almost 70 million square kilometers in size. Therefore, it is smaller than the Pacific and Atlantic oceans, but it is bigger than the Southern and Arctic oceans. At the bottom of the ocean is the Java Trench, the deepest place in the Indian Ocean. The Mid-Indian Ridge is also located on the ocean floor. The Indian Ocean is usually a calm ocean, but sometimes it has storms and tsunamis. For example, in 2004 there was an earthquake in the Indian Ocean, and many deadly tsunamis formed. These facts show how the Indian Ocean is different from all the other oceans on Earth.

Chapter 5
Earth's Atmosphere

Reading 1 – The Composition of the Atmosphere

Preparing to Read

1 Previewing key terms Page 104
A

Sample answer:

Composition means a mixture of things that join together to form something.

2 Building background knowledge about the topic Page 104
A

Sample answers: The gases that make up the atmosphere are nitrogen, oxygen, argon, carbon dioxide, water vapor, neon, helium, methane, krypton, hydrogen, ozone, and xenon.

B

1.
    1. d   2. f   3. e   4. a   5. c   6. b
2.
1. Nitrogen and oxygen make up most of Earth's atmosphere.
2. Helium makes balloons float.
3. Ozone protects life on our planet from harmful light from the sun.
4. Carbon dioxide makes soda bubbly.
5. Hydrogen is very flammable.

After You Read

1 Examining test questions Page 107
A

1. twelve
2. nitrogen and oxygen
3. nitrogen
4. ozone
5. carbon dioxide
6. the special combination of gases in the atmosphere

B

1. Our air is composed of a mixture of 12 gases: nitrogen, oxygen, argon, carbon dioxide, water vapor, neon, helium, methane, krypton, hydrogen, ozone, and xenon. (Par. 2)
2. The two main gases are nitrogen and oxygen. (Par. 2)
3. Second, humans need plants, and plants need the nitrogen in the air to grow. (Par. 3)
4. The ozone in the atmosphere also protects us. It blocks harmful rays from the sun . . . (Par. 3)
5. Carbon dioxide, for example, prevents the air from becoming too cold. (Par. 3)
6. The special combination of gases in the atmosphere allows life on Earth to exist. (Par. 3)

2 Guessing meaning from context Page 107
1. d   2. c   3. b   4. e   5. a

3 Describing parts Page 108
A

- Our air is composed of a mixture of 12 gases: nitrogen, oxygen, argon, carbon dioxide, water vapor, neon, helium, methane, krypton, hydrogen, ozone, and xenon. (Par. 2)
- The atmosphere consists of 78 percent nitrogen and 21 percent oxygen. (Par. 2)
- The other gases make up only a small percentage of the atmosphere, but they are very important. (Par. 2)

B

1. Earth's atmosphere consists of 78 percent nitrogen and 21 percent oxygen.
2. Ten gases make up less than one percent of the atmosphere.
3. The atmosphere is composed of 12 gases.
4. The atmosphere is composed of several gases that are essential for human life.
5. Oxygen makes up almost 50 percent of Earth's crust.
6. The atmosphere consists of less than one percent carbon dioxide.

4 Reviewing paragraph structure Page 108

Paragraph 3

5 Transition words Page 109
A

4   a. In addition
8   b.
3   c. Second
1   d.
2   e. First
7   f. Finally
5   g.
6   h.

Reading 2 – The Structure of the Atmosphere

Preparing to Read

2 Previewing key parts of a text Page 110

1. the different layers of the atmosphere/the structure of the atmosphere
2. five layers

3 Examining graphics Page 110
A

1. the troposphere
2. the exosphere
3. the thermosphere
4. the troposphere and the stratosphere
5. the exosphere
6. the troposphere
7. the mesosphere

After You Read

1 Taking notes with a chart Page 113
A

Layer	Name	Height (from____ to____)	Special features
1	*troposphere*	*from Earth's surface to 12 km*	• *all living things here* • *where weather conditions are*
2	*stratosphere*	*from 12 km to 50 km*	• *no wind or weather* • *ozone layer here*
3	mesosphere	*from 50 km to 80 km*	• *coldest layer* • *meteors burn up here*
4	*thermosphere*	*from 80 km to 550 km*	• *hottest layer* • *International Space Station here*
5	*exosphere*	*from 550 km to?*	• satellites in this layer • *air is very thin*

2 Playing with words Page 113

Sample answers:

1. bird (other words name nonliving things)
2. tree (other words name things that can fly)
3. spacecraft (other words name things found in nature)
4. astronaut (other words name non-human objects)
5. thunder (other words name weather conditions you can see)
6. atmosphere (other words name layers of the atmosphere)

3 Colons, *such as*, and lists Page 114
A

Lists that follow a colon:

■ Scientists divide the atmosphere into five layers: the troposphere, the stratosphere, the mesosphere, the thermosphere, and the exosphere. (Par. 1)
■ It contains all the familiar parts of our world: the oceans, the mountains, the clouds, and all living things. (Par. 2)

List that follows *such as*:

■ Most of the water in the atmosphere is located here, so weather conditions, such as rain, snow, and thunder, occur in the troposphere. (Par. 2)

B

1. There are four main types of wet weather: rain, snow, hail, and sleet.
2. There are several types of wet weather, such as rain, snow, and hail.
3. There are four main types of wet weather: rain, snow, hail, and sleet.
4. There are several types of wet weather, such as rain, snow, and hail.
5. There are several types of wet weather: rain, snow, and hail.
6. There are several types of wet weather, such as rain, snow, and hail.
7. There are many types of wet weather: rain, snow, hail, and sleet.

4 Writing about height Page 115
A

▪ The atmosphere around Earth <u>extends far above</u> the surface of the planet. (Par. 1)
▪ It <u>extends from</u> Earth's surface <u>to</u> an average of 12 kilometers <u>above</u> the surface. (Par. 2)
▪ It <u>starts at</u> 12 kilometers and <u>ends at</u> about 50 kilometers <u>above</u> Earth. (Par. 3)
▪ The mesosphere <u>extends from</u> 50 kilometers <u>to</u> 80 kilometers <u>above</u> the surface of Earth. (Par. 4)
▪ The thermosphere <u>is located</u> approximately 80 kilometers <u>above</u> Earth's surface. (Par. 5)

B

1. The <u>troposphere</u> extends <u>from</u> our planet's surface <u>to</u> an average of 12 kilometers above the surface.
2. The <u>thermosphere</u> is located 30 kilometers above the stratosphere.
3. The mesosphere <u>starts</u> at 50 kilometers and <u>ends</u> at 80 kilometers above Earth.
4. The thermosphere <u>is</u> located <u>80</u> kilometers <u>above</u> Earth.
5. Satellites <u>are located</u> hundreds of kilometers above Earth in the <u>exosphere</u>.

Reading 3 – Clouds
Preparing to Read

1 Previewing art Page 116
B

1. a. cumulus   b. cirrus   c. stratus

2. Other types of clouds include nimbus, stratus, stratocumulus, cirrocumulus, cirrostratus, cumulonimbus, altostratus, and altocumulus.
3. **Sample answers:**

   ▪ When you see fluffy, white (cumulus) clouds, the weather is usually sunny and the skies are blue.
   ▪ When you see thin, wispy (cirrus) clouds, stormy weather may be coming.
   ▪ When you see dark (stratus) clouds, it may rain or snow soon.

2 Building background knowledge about the topic Page 116
B

1. solid   2. liquid   3. gas

After You Read

1 Taking notes with a chart Page 120
Pictures will vary. **Sample answers:**

Cloud name	Description	Picture
Cumulus	• *fluffy, white* • *looks like balls of cotton* • *found 460–915 m above ground*	
Cirrus	• thin, wispy, white • looks like a thin curl of hair • found 5–12 km above ground	
Stratus	• *gray, shapeless; wide, not thick* • *looks like a blanket* • *can be close to the ground (fog)*	~~~~

2 Using symbols and abbreviations Pages 120–121
A

1. information   2. example   3. kilometer
4. plus   5. rise; increase   6. equals
7.–9. *Answers will vary.*

D

Sample answers:
Cirrus clouds

▪ thin, wispy, white
▪ usually = <u>stormy weather</u> soon
▪ high level (≈ <u>5–15 km above ground</u>)
▪ b/c cold @ high level, made of ice, not <u>water</u>
▪ cold air moves under warm air → warm air <u>rises</u> → warm air cools → <u>ice crystals</u> = <u>cirrus clouds</u>

3 Words from Latin and Greek Pages 121–122

A

Sample answers:

- Nimbostratus clouds are layers of rain clouds.
- Cirrostratus clouds are layers of curly clouds.

D

Sample answers:

1. telescope: a type of equipment that makes faraway/ distant objects look closer and bigger
2. geology: the study of rocks and the earth
3. astrometry: the measurement of stars
4. biometrics: the measurement of biological data
5. biology: the study of life and living things
6. astrophotography: taking pictures of stars
7. telephoto: a picture of an object that is far away
8. photometer: a piece of equipment that measures light

E

Sample answers: astrology, bioscope, biography, photograph, telegraph

4 *When* clauses Pages 122–123

A

- Clouds form when warm water vapor in the air rises in the atmosphere. (Par. 1)
- When you see cumulus clouds, the weather is generally good, and the sky is blue. (Par. 2)
- A cumulus cloud forms when sunshine warms water vapor in the air. (Par. 2)
- When you see cirrus clouds in the sky, it usually means that stormy weather is on its way. (Par. 3)
- A cirrus cloud forms when cold air moves under an area of warm air. (Par. 3)
- When you see stratus clouds, you might soon see rain. (Par. 4)
- A stratus cloud forms when warm, wet air moves slowly over an area of cooler air. (Par. 4)

Commas separate the *when* clause in three of the sentences. This happens when the *when* clause comes at the beginning of a sentence.

B

Sample answers:

1. When water vapor rises, a cloud forms.
2. It is probably not going to rain when you see cumulus clouds.
3. When children draw clouds, they usually draw cumulus clouds.
4. We call it fog when stratus clouds lie on the ground or ocean.
5. When you see cumulonimbus clouds, it will probably rain soon.

Chapter 5 Academic Vocabulary Review

Page 124

1. equipment
2. vehicles
3. unstable
4. stress
5. structure
6. symbol
7. finally
8. invisible
9. construction
10. enable

Developing Writing Skills

Pages 125–126

A

2. *Answers will vary.*
3. b (go 42 km/second);
   d (Meteorites – 100+ fall to Earth each yr)

B

3. **Sample paragraph:**

Auroras are beautiful, colorful lights high up in the atmosphere. They usually look green-yellow, but sometimes they are red, blue, or violet. They also appear in different shapes and sizes. Auroras form in the thermosphere, from 100 to 300 kilometers or more above Earth. They occur when particles from the sun combine with the atmospheric gases above the North and South poles. There are two famous examples of auroras. Aurora borealis (Northern Lights) is best seen from Alaska, eastern Canada, and Iceland in September, October, and March. Another example is aurora australis (Southern Lights). This aurora is best seen from Antarctica. If you are lucky, you may see an aurora one day and be able to enjoy these beautiful lights of nature in the night sky.

Chapter 6
Weather and Climate

Reading 1 – Climates Around the World

Preparing to Read

Thinking about the topic Page 127
B

Sample answers:

2.

Group 1	Group 2	Group 3
Alaska (U.S.A.)	Gobi Desert, China	Hawaii (U.S.A.)
Nord, Greenland	Sahara Desert, Africa	Puerto Rico
Northern Canada	Rub' al-Khali, Saudi Arabia	Thailand

3.

Sample answers:

Group 1: cold places
Group 2: hot and dry places
Group 3: hot and wet (tropical) places

After You Read

1 Applying what you have read Page 130

Place	Average annual temperature	Average annual precipitation	Climate
1. Manila, Philippines	27°C / 81°F	206 cm / 81.1 in	*tropical*
2. Inuvik, Canada	–9.5°C / 15°F	27 cm / 10.6 in	*polar*
3. Namib Desert, Namibia	16°C / 61°F	5 cm / 2 in	*dry*
4. Yakutsk, Russia	–10°C / 14°F	20 cm / 7.9 in	*polar*
5. Monrovia, Liberia	26°C / 79°F	513 cm / 202 in	*tropical*
6. Santiago, Chile	14°C / 57°F	38 cm / 15 in	*mild*

2 Defining key words Page 130
1. c   2. d   3. e   4. a   5. b

3 Understanding averages Page 131
B

Sample answer:

The average annual temperature in Buenos Aires, Argentina, is 16.3° Celsius (61.3° Fahrenheit).

C

Sample answer:

The average summer temperature in Amman, Jordan, is 25° Celsius (77° Fahrenheit), and the average summer temperature in Buenos Aires, Argentina, is 22.3° Celsius (72.1° Fahrenheit).

4 Introducing examples Page 132
A

- For example, <u>tropical rain forests grow in hot, wet climates, and polar bears live in cold climates.</u> (Par. 1)
- For example, <u>San Francisco and London are cities with mild climates.</u> (Par. 3)
- For example, <u>air and ocean temperatures have been rising in recent years.</u> (Par. 4)
- Scientists believe that global warming is causing other climate changes on our planet, such as <u>an increase in heat waves and more powerful storms all over the world.</u> (Par. 4)

C

Our planet is getting warmer. Some temperature change is natural. However, temperatures on Earth increased much faster than expected in recent years. <u>For example, over the 100 years of the twentieth century, temperatures increased by 0.5°C. However, before that time, it took 400 years for temperatures to increase by the same amount.</u>

Global warming is causing some troubling climate changes. <u>For example, some areas are having more heat waves, others are getting heavier rain, and polar areas are getting warmer.</u> Unfortunately, people around the world are adding to the problem. They are using more and more energy for heat, electricity, and transportation. Burning fossil fuels, <u>such as oil, gas, and coal</u>, produces most of this energy, and this increases global warming. To slow global warming and help prevent further damage to the planet, people need to make some changes in their daily lives. <u>For example, they could recycle more things, walk more, and drive less.</u>

Reading 2 – Storms

Preparing to Read

Previewing key parts of a text Page 133

A

1. descriptions and statistics for two types of storms
2. a. thunderstorms   b. tornadoes

B

1. F   2. T   3. T   4. F

After You Read

1 Using a Venn diagram to organize ideas from a text Page 136

A

TO	are fast moving
TO	can lift houses into the air
B	can cause a lot of damage
TH	can produce lightning and hail
TO	are tall, spinning clouds
B	happen throughout the world
TH	happen more than 1,000 times a day
TH	can cause dangerous flooding

B

Thunderstorms	Both	Tornadoes
• happen more than 1,000 times a day	• can cause a lot of damage	• are fast moving
• can produce lightning and hail	• happen throughout the world	• are tall, spinning clouds
• can cause dangerous flooding		• can lift houses into the air

2 Using a dictionary Page 137

Sample answers:

1. short: (adj.) happening for only a small amount of time
2. last: (v.) to continue for a period of time; to continue to exist
3. over: (prep.) more than
4. over: (adj.) finished, completed, or ended
5. strike: (v.) to happen suddenly

3 Using *this / that / these / those* to connect ideas Page 138

Sample answers:

1. Phrase: This movement of air
   Refers to: The hot air expands. Then quickly contracts . . .
2. Phrase: These short thunderstorms
   Refers to: Approximately 90 percent of thunderstorms . . .
3. Phrase: this area
   Refers to: "Tornado Alley," an area in the central part of the country
4. Phrase: these destructive storms
   Refers to: severe thunderstorms and tornadoes

4 Examining statistics Page 139
A
Sample answers:

- almost 2,000 thunderstorms (Par. 1)
- Approximately 90 percent of thunderstorms (Par. 2)
- no longer than 30 minutes (Par. 2)
- over 7,000 forest fires (Par. 2)
- more than 90 deaths (Par. 2)
- almost $1 billion of damage (Par. 2)
- 15 minutes or less (Par. 3)
- more than 480 kilometers per hour (Par. 3)
- more than 1,000 tornadoes (Par. 4)
- more than 100 tornadoes (Par. 4)

B
1. b   2. a   3. c   4. b   5. b   6. a

Reading 3 – Hurricanes

Preparing to Read

2 Increasing reading speed Page 140
C
1. warm waters (Par. 2)
2. three (Par. 3)
3. damage (Par. 4)
4. deadly and costly (Par. 5)
5. more (Par. 6)

After You Read

1 Reading for main ideas Page 143
A

1. Par. 3   4. Par. 4
2. Par. 6   5. Par. 5
3. Par. 1   6. Par. 2

B
3

2 Synonyms Page 143
B

1. refer   4. damage
2. starts   5. devastating
3. powerful

C
Sample answers:

- The test begins at 9:00. It always starts on time, so don't be late.
- Frogs have strong legs. They can use their powerful legs to jump very high.

3 Prepositions of location Page 144
A
1. Hurricanes form near the equator.
2. Some hurricanes form over the warm waters of the Gulf of Mexico.
3. The eye of a hurricane is in the middle of the spinning storm.
4. Rain bands circle around the eye of the hurricane.

Diagrams will vary.

4 Thinking critically about the topic Page 145
Sample answers:

1. Temperatures are increasing; there have been more storms lately; storms have been more severe; some places are getting too much rain, and others are not getting enough.
2. To help slow global warming, we can drive less and take public transportation more, use air-conditioning less often, and turn off lights and electric appliances when they are not in use.
3. Some reasons why people, companies, and countries have not made changes to slow global warming: People are lazy; they don't care about the problem; they don't know what to do; in some cases, it is too expensive to make changes.

Chapter 6 Academic Vocabulary Review

Page 146

1. global   6. injuries
2. located   7. approximately
3. benefits   8. period
4. research   9. consists
5. expand   10. generate

Practicing Academic Writing

Preparing to Write

2 Using specific support in your writing Page 149
D

Sample paragraph:

Nor'easters are powerful storms that occur along the east coast of the United States. Winds that blow from the northeast create these storms, which usually take place between October and April. Nor'easters can be dangerous and can cause many problems. For example, they can produce heavy snow, rain, winds, and giant waves with flooding. Nor'easters can even kill people. Some Nor'easters, such as the Blizzard of 1978, become so famous that people talk about them for years. The Blizzard of 1978 was a powerful storm that struck the state of Massachusetts and caused a lot of damage and death. When the storm ended, more than 30 hours after it started, there were almost 70 centimeters of snow on the ground in the city of Boston. This destructive nor'easter destroyed more than 2,000 houses and damaged almost 10,000 more. It caused over $500 million of damage. More than 70 people died in the storm, and approximately 17,000 people had to go to emergency shelters.

Now Write

Page 150

A

Sample paragraph:

Taichung's Climate

The climate in Taichung, Taiwan, is hot and humid in the summer, cooler in the winter, and sometimes rainy. During the hottest months of July, August, and September, temperatures can reach 33°C. However, in the winter months of January and February it is cooler. For example, last winter the temperature dropped as low as 22°C. The rest of the year, the temperatures are very comfortable. Another important feature of the climate in Taichung is the heavy rain that the monsoon winds bring in June, July, and August. During the rainy season, it often rains for more than a month without stopping. In an average year, about 162 centimeters of rainfall, and more than half of that rain falls during the rainy season. In Taichung, it is very hot and rainy at times, but most of the year, the weather is good.

Chapter 7
Plants and Animals

Previewing the Unit

Chapter 7: Plants and Animals Page 153
B

1. P   2. A   3. A   4. P   5. A   6. P

Chapter 8: Humans Page 153
A

1. T   2. F   3. T   4. F   5. F   6. T

B

a. muscular system   b. skeletal (bone) system

Reading 1 – Living Things

Preparing to Read

1 Thinking about the topic Page 154
A

2 and 6 are false; all others true.

C

Sample answers:

- All living things are made of cells.
- All living things reproduce (produce young).

2 Building background knowledge about the topic Page 154
B

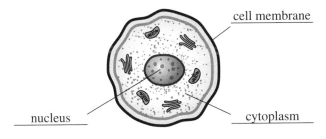

After You Read

1 Answering true/false questions Page 157
A

F	1. Par. 2		F	5. Par. 3
T	2. Par. 2		F	6. Par. 1
T	3. Par. 5		T	7. Par. 3
F	4. Par. 4		T	8. Par. 4

B

1. All organisms need water.
4. Humans are multicellular organisms, but bacteria are single-celled organisms.
5. All cells have a cell membrane and cytoplasm, and most cells have a nucleus.
6. Fish and birds are organisms, but rocks are not.

2 Word families Page 157
A

1. life (n.) living (adj.) (Par. 1, 6)
2. difference (n.) different (adj.) (Par. 5)
3. similarity (n.) similar (adj.) (Par. 2)
4. cell (n.) multicellular (adj.) (Par. 4, 5)
5. movement (n.) move (v.) (Par. 3)
6. diversity (n.) diverse (adj.) (Par. 2)

B

1. different
2. cell
3. move
4. similar
5. diversity

3 Asking for clarification Page 158

B

Sample answers:

1. In other words, a cell is the smallest living thing on Earth.
2. The word *circulatory* describes something that moves in a circle.
3. Some examples of organ systems are the digestive system, the respiratory system, the nervous system, the skeletal system, and the muscular system.
4. "All organisms develop" means that all organisms grow and change.

C

Sample answers:

- Could you explain what the word *nucleus* means? (A nucleus is the central part of a cell; it contains all the information a cell needs to grow and develop.)
- I don't understand what the text means in paragraph 2 where it says that life on Earth is extremely diverse. (It means that living things on Earth are not all the same. They differ in many ways, including size, shape, and habitat.)

4 Writing about similarities Pages 159–160

A

Par. 1: They <u>are all</u> organisms, or living things, . . .
Par. 2: Although organisms are different from each other in these ways, they are <u>similar</u> in other ways. For example, they <u>all</u> need water, ... In addition, <u>all</u> organisms grow, develop, and eventually die.
Par. 3: <u>Another important similarity is that all</u> organisms <u>are</u> composed of cells . . . . <u>All</u> cells have an outer covering, called a cell membrane.
Par. 4: For example, <u>both</u> bacteria and algae <u>are</u> single-celled organisms.

B

1. similar; similarity, all
2. both
3. Both
4. All

C

Sample answers:

1. Both dogs and cats have tails.
2. One similarity is that whales and fish both live in water.
3. Mosquitoes and ants are both insects.

D

1. The writer is comparing lions and tigers.
2. The three points of comparison are diet, family group, and size.
3. Lions and tigers <u>are similar</u> in three ways. <u>One similarity is</u> the food they eat. Lions and tigers are <u>both</u> meat eaters that hunt other large and medium-size animals. <u>Another similarity is that both</u> animals <u>are</u> part of the cat family. Lions <u>are</u> also <u>similar to</u> tigers in size. <u>Both</u> animals <u>are</u> about <u>the same</u> weight and height.

E

Sample paragraph:

Dogs and cats are similar in several ways. First, both animals are popular house pets. They are both good companions for people. Another similarity is that dogs and cats have some physical features in common. For example, they both have hair, whiskers, four legs, and a tail. In addition, dogs and cats both eat meat. These are just a few examples of how dogs and cats are similar.

Reading 2 – Plant Life

Preparing to Read

1 Conducting a survey Page 161

A

Sample answers:

- Reasons that plants are important include the following: They give us oxygen; they are a source of food for people and animals; they are beautiful; and they make people happy.
- Products we get from plants include cotton clothing, pencils, paper, fruits, vegetables, herbs, rice and other grains, wooden furniture, linen tablecloths, chocolate, and coffee.

2 Previewing key parts of a text Page 161

B

1. T   2. F   3. T   4. F   5. T

After You Read

1 Making an outline Page 164

I. Diversity of plants
  A. ≈ 300,000 types of plants on Earth
  B. grow in lots of different <u>climates</u>
II. Plant size and structure
  A. different sizes
  B. plant structure: made up of <u>cells</u>, which have cell <u>membranes</u>, <u>cytoplasm</u>, a <u>nucleus</u>, and cell <u>walls</u>
III. Seedless plants
  A. grow from <u>spores</u>, not seeds
  B. do not have flowers and most grow in <u>damp</u> places
IV. <u>Seed plants</u>
  A. more common than seedless plants
  B. they have <u>roots</u>, <u>stems</u>, and <u>leaves</u>, and they can have <u>flowers</u>
V. Products from plants
  A. provide us with food, clothing, paper, wood, and medicine
  B. most importantly, they provide <u>oxygen</u>
VI. Photosynthesis
  A. takes place in plant leaves
  B. the process: plants take in <u>sunlight</u>, <u>carbon dioxide</u>, and <u>water</u>, and they make <u>glucose</u>
  C. process puts <u>oxygen</u> into the air and takes out <u>carbon dioxide</u>
VII. Plant loss
  A. causes: <u>natural disasters, such as fires; human activities, such as deforestation</u>
  B. effects: <u>plants and animals lose their habitats; drought; less oxygen in air; more carbon dioxide contributes to global warming</u>

2 Defining key words Page 165
A

1. d   2. c   3. a   4. e   5. f   6. b

B

flower
leaves
stem
roots

C

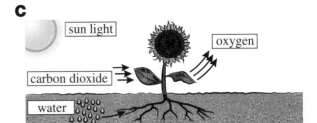

sun light
oxygen
carbon dioxide
water

Photosynthesis

3 Cues for finding word meaning Page 166

Word		Definition	Clue
1. spores	(Par. 3)	*tiny cells that grow into new plants*	*Spores are . . .*
2. photosynthesis	(Par. 6)	*a plant's food-making process*	*. . . , called photosynthesis*
3. glucose	(Par. 6)	*a kind of sugar*	*Glucose is . . .*
4. deforestation	(Par. 7)	*destruction of trees*	*deforestation, or . . .*
5. drought	(Par. 7)	*a long period of time without rain*	*drought ( )*

4 Writing about differences Pages 167–168
A

Par. 1: Plants are similar to other organisms in several ways, <u>but</u> they also have their own special features.
Par. 2: <u>In contrast</u>, you cannot see the top of some of the giant redwood trees in northern California . . .
  <u>One difference</u> is that plant cells also have a thick, rigid cell wall . . .
Par. 4: <u>Unlike</u> seedless plants, many also have flowers.

B

1. different
2. In contrast
3. difference
4. but
5. Unlike

C

Sample answers:

Roses have beautiful flowers, but moss does not have any flowers.

Roses grow from seeds. In contrast, moss grows from spores.

Unlike roses, moss often grows on rocks.

One difference between roses and moss is that roses need sun, but moss needs shade.

D

1. The writer is contrasting the cacao tree and the deadly nightshade plant.
2. The three points of contrast are location, appearance, and fruit.
3. There are several differences between the cacao tree and the plant called deadly nightshade. One difference is the places where they grow. Cacao trees grow in Central and South America. In contrast, nightshade grows in parts of Europe, Africa, Asia, and North America. The cacao tree and nightshade also look very different. The cacao tree grows about eight meters high, but nightshade grows only to about one meter. The most important difference between the cacao tree and nightshade is in the fruit they produce. Cacao trees produce huge berries called cacao pods. Inside the pods are the seeds that are used to make chocolate. Unlike the cacao fruit, nightshade berries are poisonous and can be fatal when eaten. As you can see, nightshade and the cacao tree are two very different plants.

E

Sample paragraph:

There are several differences between basil plants and pansies. One important difference is the conditions they need to grow. Pansies grow best when the weather is cool. In fact, pansies can continue to grow even when it snows lightly. In contrast, basil needs hot, dry weather, and it will die if it gets too cold. Another difference between basil and pansies is the flowers. Basil plants produce long white or purple flowers with many petals. Unlike basil, pansies come in many different colors, such as yellow, orange, purple, red, and white. Each flower has only five petals. The biggest difference between the two plants is that basil is an herb, but a pansy is not. People often use basil leaves in cooking, but they use pansies to provide color in the garden. Although basil and pansies are both popular garden plants, they look very different, and they have different needs and uses.

Reading 3 – Animal Life

Preparing to Read

Thinking about the topic Page 169

A

Sample answers:

1. Groupings
- animals in the air: bird, mosquito
- animals in the water: crab, fish, turtle, whale
- animals on land: cow, dog, elephant, kangaroo, ladybug, lion, monkey, mouse, spider, worm
- animals on land and in the water: crab, turtle

2. Regroupings
- big animals: cow, elephant, kangaroo, lion, monkey, whale
- medium-size animals: dog, monkey
- small animals: bird, crab, ladybug, mosquito, mouse, spider, turtle, worm

B

Sample answers:

1. In photo a, the rhinoceros and the birds are friends.
2. In photo b, the turtle and the fish like to travel together.
3. In photo c, the mosquito is biting/hurting the person.

After You Read

1 Applying what you have read Page 172
A

1. V (chimpanzee)
2. V (snake)
3. V (eagle)
4. V (horse)
5. I (crab)
6. I (snail)
7. V (fish)
8. I (shrimp)

B

1. M   2. C   3. P   4. M   5. P

C

1. extinct   2. endangered

2 *That* clauses Page 173
A

Sample answers:

- Vertebrates are animals that have a backbone. (Par. 2)
- A backbone is a line of bones that goes down the middle of the animal's back. (Par. 2)
- The spinal cord is an important group of nerves that send messages between the brain and the rest of the body. (Par. 2)
- Invertebrates are animals that do not have backbones, such as worms and spiders. (Par. 3)
- For example, some small birds sit on water buffaloes and eat the insects that bother the animals. (Par. 5)
- For example, a fly may land on a cow that is walking across a field. (Par. 5)

B

Sample answers:

1. Plants are organisms that can make their own food.
2. Birds are animals that have feathers and can fly.
3. Human activities cause environmental changes that sometimes hurt other living things on our planet.
4. Some animals form relationships that they both benefit from.
5. Earth is a planet that has more saltwater than freshwater.

3 Compound words Pages 173–174
A

Sample answers:

1. a bone that goes down your back
2. a fish that is soft and squishy (like jelly)
3. a tree that has red wood
4. a horse that runs in races
5. a lot of ideas coming quickly in a person's brain
6. the top of a mountain
7. a boat that people can live on
8. a chair that has arms
9. a thick substance that cleans teeth

B

Sample answers:

songbird, earthquake, earthworm, rainfall, rainwater, sunshine, sunflower, shellfish, thunderstorm, waterfall

4 Writing about similarities and differences Pages 174–175
A

1. The writer compares and contrasts sharks and jellyfish.
2. similarities: Both live in the ocean; both can hurt people and other animals.
   differences: Sharks are vertebrates, but jellyfish are invertebrates; sharks live longer than jellyfish.
3. Although there are similarities between these animals, there are also important differences.
4. Sharks and jellyfish are <u>similar to, and different from, each other</u> in several ways. <u>One similarity is that both</u> animals live in the ocean. <u>Another similarity is that both</u> sharks and jellyfish can hurt people and other animals. A shark can bite with its sharp teeth, and a jellyfish can sting with its tentacles. Although <u>there are similarities between</u> these animals, <u>there are also important differences.</u> <u>One difference is that</u> sharks are vertebrates and jellyfish are invertebrates. This means that, <u>unlike</u> sharks, jellyfish do not have backbones or brains. Sharks and jellyfish also <u>have different</u> life spans. Most jellyfish live only a few months. <u>In contrast,</u> most sharks live 15–20 years. These facts show that sharks and jellyfish <u>are similar and different</u> at the same time.

B

Sample paragraph:

Cheetahs and Giraffes

Cheetahs and giraffes are two mammals that have many differences and a few similarities. The clearest difference between the cheetah and the giraffe is the size and shape of their bodies. The giraffe is the tallest animal on land. An average giraffe is about 5 meters tall. In contrast, an average cheetah is about 80 centimeters tall, but its long body and powerful legs make it the fastest animal on land. In fact, cheetahs can run as fast as 112 kilometers an hour. Another difference between the two animals is their diet. Giraffes are herbivores, which means they do not eat meat. Their favorite food is the leaves of the acacia tree. Unlike giraffes, cheetahs are meat eaters. They usually eat antelopes, birds, and rabbits. Although these two animals are very different, they do have a few things in common. One similarity is the place where they live. Both giraffes and cheetahs live in Africa. Another similarity is that both animals have short fur. In addition, they both have spots on their fur. As you can see, the giraffe and the cheetah are very different from each other, but they have a few similar features.

5 Thinking critically about the topic Page 175

A

Sample answers:

1. Some endangered animals are Asian elephants, blue whales, gorillas, giant pandas, red wolves, Siberian tigers, and California condors. Some extinct animals are dodo birds, saber-toothed tigers, wooly mammoths, giant kangaroos, giant moas, dinosaurs, Irish deer, and Caspian tigers.
2. Animals may become endangered or extinct because people kill them for food or fur, or because people think the animals are pests.

B

1. *Answers will vary.*
2. Animal communication techniques include making noises (barking, meowing, growling); touching each other with their paws, noses, or faces; and bringing things to each other, such as food or toys.
3. Some ways animals communicate with people include making noise, wagging their tails, staring, and bringing people things.

C

Dolphins communicate with each other in their own language, which people cannot understand.

Chapter 7 Academic Vocabulary Review

Page 176

1. release
2. communicate
3. survival
4. establish
5. attach
6. transport
7. contributes
8. techniques
9. categories
10. structure

Developing Writing Skills

Pages 177–178

A

1. F   2. T   3. T   4. T   5. T and F

B

Sample answer:

It is true because humans and plants are both living things, so they both belong to the same class (living things). It is false because living things can also be divided into two different categories: plant life and animal life. In that case, humans and plants are not in the same class.

C

Sample answers:

1. Mammals and amphibians both have a backbone and a skeleton inside their body.
2. Mammals are warm-blooded, but amphibians are cold-blooded. Unlike mammals, amphibians lay eggs. Mammals take care of their babies, but amphibian babies take care of themselves.
3. Mammals and amphibians are both categorized as vertebrates because they both have a backbone.

D

2.
   1. plants
   2. vascular and nonvascular
   3. how plants get water

3.

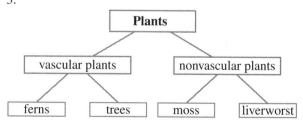

Chapter 8
Humans

Reading 1 – The Brain

Preparing to Read

Thinking about the topic Page 179
A

Sample answers:

Humans are unique because they are very intelligent, they have a complex language system, and they know they will die someday.

B

The picture shows a woman's face/a man playing the saxophone.

After You Read

1 Highlighting and taking notes Page 182
A

1. The main idea is highlighted in gray; the details are highlighted in yellow.
2. and 3. *Answers will vary*

B

Answers will vary. Check to make sure that students have limited their highlighting to important information.

2 Using adjectives Page 183
A

Phineas Gage was a <u>railroad</u> employee. He was a <u>good</u> worker and a <u>respected</u> man. His employer and employees liked him. Phineas was <u>smart</u> and <u>responsible</u>, and he was a <u>fair</u> boss. One day in 1848, there was a <u>terrible</u> accident. A <u>heavy iron</u> bar went right through Gage's head. Surprisingly, he did not die, but a <u>large</u> section of the <u>front</u> part of his brain was destroyed.

Phineas's personality changed dramatically. When he went back to work the <u>next</u> year, everyone noticed <u>enormous</u> changes. Before the accident, Gage was <u>calm</u>, <u>hardworking</u>, <u>responsible</u>, and <u>friendly</u>. However, after the accident, he became <u>angry</u>, <u>childish</u>, <u>rude</u>, and <u>impatient</u>. Friends said they did not know this Phineas. For <u>many</u> years, scientists discussed Phineas Gage and the roles of the mind and the brain. Could damage to a <u>certain</u> part of the brain affect personality? Years later, scientists discovered that the <u>front</u> part of the brain controls personality. This explains why Gage's personality changed so much after his injury.

B

Sample answers:

1. The brain is a small organ.
2. Humans have complex brains.
3. There are different types of seedless plants on Earth.
4. Mosquitoes are annoying insects.
5. Elephants are enormous and intelligent animals.

C

Sample answers:

It is the tallest animal on land. It has a long neck, four long legs, and a very long tongue. Its fur is yellow with brown spots. (a giraffe)

3 Gerunds Page 184

A

__G__ 1. <u>Thinking</u> is something our brains do all day long.

_____ 2. Many scientists are <u>doing</u> brain research.

__G__ 3. Experts say that <u>sleeping</u> is very important for healthy brain development.

__G__ 4. <u>Hearing</u> and <u>seeing</u> are two senses that the brain controls.

_____ 5. Scientists are <u>learning</u> more about the brain every day.

B

Sample answers:

1. The cerebrum controls most of a person's <u>thinking</u> and <u>speaking</u>.

2. The right hemisphere of the brain is important for creative abilities, such as <u>drawing</u> and <u>painting</u>.

3. The brain stem controls some of the body's basic functions, such as <u>breathing</u>.

5 Writing a description page 186

A

1. and 2.
The ___ is ⬭small⬭ and ⬭complex⬭. An average ___ is about <u>the size of two fists, and it</u> <u>weighs approximately 1.4 kilograms</u>. Some people describe the ___ as looking like a ⬭soft⬭, ⬭pink⬭, ⬭wrinkled⬭ rock. Others say it looks like a <u>sponge</u> . . .

3. The writer is describing the brain.

C

Sample paragraph:

   The human eye is round, and it is about 2.5 centimeters from side to side and top to bottom. A large part of the eye is white. In the middle of the white part is a smaller circle. This circle can be brown, green, or blue. Inside the colored circle is a smaller black circle. The eye can move up and down and side to side when it looks in different directions. Over the eye is the eyelid, which is the skin that covers the eye when it closes.

Reading 2 – The Skeletal and Muscular Systems

Preparing to Read

1 Thinking about the topic Page 187

1. B	5. B/M
2. B/M	6. B
3. M	7. B
4. B/M	8. M

2 Increasing reading speed Page 187

C

1. 206	4. more muscles than bones
2. support the body	5. cannot
3. help the body move	

After You Read

1 Asking and answering questions about a text Page 190

A

Sample answers:

1. Body movements include walking, talking, sitting, bending, blinking, and smiling.

2. Muscles and bones allow us to move.

3. A skeleton is a framework of bones inside the body. It gives the body shape and support.

4. A bone is made of living cells and tissues; it is lightweight and strong; the outside is hard, and the inside has some empty spaces.

5. Two purposes of bones are to protect internal organs and to help support the body.

6. The femur is a bone that supports the weight of the body as we walk and run.

2 Highlighting and taking notes Page 190

A

Sample answers:

<u>Bones</u> have two main purposes. Some bones protect the internal organs. For example, the skull bones protect the brain, the ribs protect the heart, and the backbone protects the spinal cord. Other bones, such as the femur, or thighbone, help support the body. The femur is the longest bone in the body. It is an average of 48 centimeters long, and it supports the weight of the body as we walk and run.

skull ribs backbone → protect the internal organs

femur → help support the body

B

Sample answers:

Two main purposes of bones
1. To protect the body's internal organs
   - skull protects the brain
   - ribs protect the heart
   - backbone protects the spinal cord
2. To help support the body
   - femur supports body weight as we walk & run

3 Scanning for details Page 191

1. 5,000 (Par. 1)
2. 206 (Par. 2)
3. about 10 kilograms (Par. 2)
4. the femur; about 48 centimeters (Par. 3)
5. more than 600 (Par. 5)
6. to frown (Par. 5)
7. milk, beans, dark leafy green vegetables; lean meats and fish (Par. 6)
8. 2011 (Boxed text)

4 Using a dictionary Page 191

Sample answers:

1. steps: (n.) the distances covered by lifting one foot and putting it down in front of the other foot
2. tissue: (n.) a group of related cells that forms larger parts of animals and plants
3. contract: (v.) to make or become shorter or narrower, or smaller
4. relax: (v.) to become or cause a muscle or the body to become less tight
5. major: (adj.) more important, bigger, or more serious than others of the same type
6. diet: (n.) the food and drink usually taken by a person or group

5 Words that can be used as nouns or verbs Page 192

B

Sample answers:

1. The femur **supports** the body when we run.
2. Doctors listen to a patient's heart as it **beats** to make sure it is healthy.

C

Sample answers:

- I wish I had better **control** over the weeds in my garden. (noun)
  It's hard to **control** the weeds in my garden. (verb)
- A **frown** shows people that you are not happy. (noun)
  When you **frown**, people can see you are not happy. (verb)
- I like to take a **walk** with my family every night after dinner. (noun)
  I **walk** every night after dinner with my family. (verb)
- I enjoy my **work** in the chemistry lab at school. (noun)
  I **work** in the chemistry lab at school. (verb)

6 Writing about the body Page 192
A

Paragraph 2 describes bones:
Inside the body is a framework of 206 bones, called a skeleton. Bones are <u>made of living cells and tissue,</u> and they give shape and support to the body. They are both <u>lightweight</u> and <u>strong</u>. The <u>outside of a bone is hard and solid,</u> and the <u>inside has some empty spaces.</u> The empty spaces <u>make the bone weigh less.</u> An average skeleton <u>weighs only about 10 kilograms,</u> but it is <u>strong</u> enough to support the body and hold it <u>upright.</u>

This excerpt from paragraph 3 describes the femur:
. . . Other bones, such as the femur, or thighbone, help support the body. The femur is the <u>longest bone in the body.</u> It is an average of <u>48 centimeters long,</u> and it supports the weight of the body as we walk and run.

Reading 3 – The Heart and the Circulatory System

Preparing to Read

1 Building background knowledge about the topic Page 193
B

Sample answers:

1. The circulatory system transports materials to and from all the cells in the body.
2. The three main parts of the circulatory system are blood, the heart, and blood vessels. The heart pumps blood through the body. Blood vessels are small tubes that the blood travels through. Blood delivers oxygen, water, and nutrients, and it picks up waste products.

2 Conducting an experiment Page 193

Answers will vary. (An average resting pulse rate is between 60 and 100 beats per minute. After running in place, pulse rates will be higher than resting rates.)

After You Read

1 Answering multiple-choice questions Page 196

1. b
2. d
3. d
4. b
5. a
6. d
7. a
8. c
9. c
10. b

2 Sequencing Page 197
A

5	Blood flows to the left ventricle.
7	Blood returns to the heart through the right atrium.
2	Blood flows to the right ventricle.
3	Blood travels through the pulmonary artery to the lungs.
1	Blood enters the heart through the right atrium.
6	Blood travels through the aorta to all parts of the body.
4	Blood picks up oxygen and returns to the heart through the left atrium.

B

The arrows drawn on the diagram should follow the path shown in Figure 8.3 on Student's Book page 194.

3 Highlighting and making an outline Pages 197–198
A

Main ideas are underlined once; details are underlined twice.

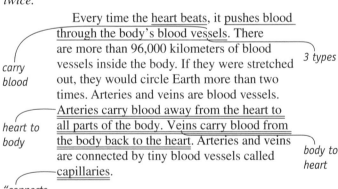

Every time the <u>heart beats</u>, it <u>pushes blood through the body's blood vessels.</u> There are more than 96,000 kilometers of blood vessels inside the body. If they were stretched out, they would circle Earth more than two times. Arteries and veins are blood vessels. <u><u>Arteries carry blood away from the heart to all parts of the body. Veins carry blood from the body back to the heart.</u></u> Arteries and veins are connected by tiny blood vessels called <u>capillaries.</u>

carry blood

heart to body

3 types

body to heart

"connects arteries + veins"

B

Sample answers:

III. Blood vessels
    A. Arteries: <u>carry blood away from heart to body</u>
    B. <u>Veins: carry blood from body back to heart</u>
    C. <u>Capillaries: connect arteries & veins</u>

C

Main ideas are underlined once; details are underlined twice.

        Your heart works hard. It started beating before you were born, and it will continue to beat for your whole life. A <u>healthy heart</u> has a <u>strong heart muscle</u> and <u>clean, open arteries</u>. <u>Blocked arteries</u> that supply blood to the heart <u>can cause a heart attack</u>. According to research, <u>smoking</u> can be <u>dangerous</u> to the heart. <u>Exercise</u> and a <u>good diet</u> also help keep the <u>heart in good shape</u>.

strong heart muscle + clean arteries

bad for heart

good for heart

VI. Heart health
    A. Healthy heart = <u>strong heart muscle & clean, open arteries</u>
    B. <u>Blocked arteries can → heart attack</u>
    C. <u>To keep heart healthy: don't smoke, do exercise, eat good diet</u>

4 Prepositions of direction Pages 198–199

A

Par. 4: . . . The flow of blood works this way: Blood <u>from</u> all over the body enters the heart <u>through</u> the top right chamber, called the right atrium. This blood flows <u>to</u> the bottom right chamber, called the right ventricle. The heart then pumps the blood <u>out of</u> the right ventricle, <u>through</u> the pulmonary artery, <u>into</u> the lungs.

Par. 5: The blood picks up oxygen in the lungs. Then it returns <u>to</u> the heart <u>through</u> the left atrium. Next, it flows <u>to</u> the left ventricle. The heart then pumps the blood <u>out of</u> the left ventricle <u>into</u> the aorta, the largest artery in the body. The blood travels <u>through</u> the aorta and other smaller arteries <u>to</u> all parts of the body and delivers oxygen <u>to</u> all the cells. The blood then travels <u>through</u> capillaries <u>to</u> veins that lead back to the heart. <u>From</u> the veins, the blood goes <u>into</u> the right atrium of the heart to begin the process again. The whole cycle takes about 30 seconds.

B

1. Arteries carry blood away <u>from</u> the heart <u>to</u> all parts of the body.
2. Blood travels <u>through</u> blood vessels.
3. Blood carries oxygen <u>from</u> the lungs <u>to</u> all the cells in the body.
4. Dr. Barnard transplanted a new heart <u>into</u> the body of Louis Washkansky.
5. Blood travels <u>through</u> capillaries <u>to</u> veins.
6. The heart pumps blood <u>out of</u> the left ventricle and <u>into</u> the aorta.

C

Sample answers:

1. The brain receives messages from the body through the spinal cord.
2. The eyes send messages from the outside world to the brain.
3. The lungs receive blood from the heart.
4. Blood carries nutrients to the body's cells.

5 Playing with words Page 199

Sample answers:

1. bones (other words name parts of the circulatory system)
2. lungs (other words name materials that blood delivers to the body's cells)
3. aorta (other words name chambers of the heart)
4. body (other words name organs)
5. blood (other words name blood vessels)
6. smoking (other words name things that are good for the heart)

6 Writing a description Page 199

A

Sample answers:

Key features of the heart	Notes
size	*about as big as a fist*
weight	*about 300 grams*
color	*mostly red*
main parts	*right atrium, right ventricle, left atrium, left ventricle*

B

Sample paragraph:

Even though it is a very important organ, the human heart's appearance is quite ordinary. The heart is not large. In fact, it is about as big as a fist and weighs about 300 grams. Just like other muscles in the body, the heart is mostly red in color. It has four main parts: the right atrium, the right ventricle, the left atrium, and the left ventricle.

Chapter 8 Academic Vocabulary Review

Page 200

1. unique
2. coordination
3. automatically
4. medical
5. voluntary
6. internal
7. computer
8. logic
9. framework
10. reject

Practicing Academic Writing

Preparing to Write

Classifying and describing Pages 202–203

A

2. Sample answers:
   Paragraph a: 1. systems of Earth; 2. interconnected systems: lithosphere, hydrosphere, atmosphere, and biosphere; 3. by definition and description of one system, lithosphere, with facts and details
   Paragraph b: 1. invertebrates; 2. worms and spiders; 3. by definition, statistics, description and details, and home or location
   Paragraph c: 1. muscles; 2. voluntary muscles; 3. by definition, facts, purpose/function, details, examples, and contrast
3. *Answers will vary.*
4. Sample answers:
   1. All nine methods are used.
   2. The descriptions are exact because of descriptive adjectives, facts, and statistics.

Now Write

Page 203

A

Answers will vary. Check that the paragraphs include a variety of descriptive methods as listed on page 202 of the Student Book.

Unit 1 • Content Quiz

Part 1 True/False questions (25 points)

Decide if the following statements are true (T) or false (F).

_____ 1. Terrestrial planets are made of gases.

_____ 2. The hydrosphere is all the water on Earth.

_____ 3. The three main types of rocks are lava, magma, and igneous.

_____ 4. Extinct volcanoes can erupt in the future.

_____ 5. Scientists cannot predict or stop earthquakes.

Part 2 Multiple choice questions (25 points)

Circle the best answer from the choices listed.

1. The sun is a _____.

   a. planet

   b. star

   c. moon

   d. plutoid

2. All the living things on Earth are part of the _____.

   a. lithosphere

   b. hydrosphere

   c. atmosphere

   d. biosphere

3. At convergent boundaries _____.

   a. tectonic plates move past each other

   b. tectonic plates stop moving

   c. tectonic plates move toward each other

   d. tectonic plates move away from each other

4. Most volcanoes are located _____.

   a. in the Atlantic Ocean

   b. around the Pacific Plate

   c. in California

   d. over hotspots

5. Earthquakes are caused by _____.

    a. tectonic plate movement

    b. human behavior

    c. rocks on Earth's surface

    d. shaking buildings

Part 3 Short answer questions (50 points)

Write a short answer to each of the following questions. In most cases no more than one or two sentences are required.

1. Describe our solar system.

2. Give an example of how Earth's systems are interconnected.

3. Choose one type of rock and explain how it forms.

4. Explain Wegener's continental drift theory.

5. Name one positive and one negative effect of volcanoes.

Name: _____

Date: _____

Unit 2 • Content Quiz

Part 1 True/False questions (25 points)

Decide if the following statements are true (T) or false (F).

_____ 1. Water covers about 50 percent of our planet.

_____ 2. Glaciers do not move.

_____ 3. The amount of salinity in an ocean depends on the amount of evaporation and the amount of freshwater added.

_____ 4. Wind causes surface currents.

_____ 5. Tsunamis are warm ocean currents.

Part 2 Multiple choice questions (25 points)

Circle the best answer from the choices listed.

1. Which one of the following is not a step in the water cycle?

    a. precipitation

    b. eruption

    c. condensation

    d. evaporation

2. Which one of the following is true about rivers?

    a. They are surrounded on all sides by land.

    b. They are an important source of salt water.

    c. They are also called aquifers.

    d. They carve V-shaped valleys.

3. Which one of the following is the smallest ocean?

    a. the Arctic Ocean

    b. the Atlantic Ocean

    c. the Indian Ocean

    d. the Pacific Ocean

4. Which one of the following is not true about currents?

    a. They stop warm water from becoming too hot.

    b. They stop cold water from becoming too cold.

    c. They always move from east to west.

    d. They can influence climate.

5. Tsunamis

    a. are caused by wind.

    b. move slowly.

    c. happen only in the Pacific Ocean.

    d. can kill people.

Part 3 Short answer questions (50 points)

Write a short answer to each of the following questions. In most cases no more than one or two sentences are required.

1. Billions of people live on our planet, and they use a lot of water every day. Why don't we ever run out of water?

2. Explain one similarity and one difference between a river and an ocean.

3. How does a glacier form?

4. Why does ocean water near the equator usually have high levels of salinity?

5. What is a tsunami?

Name: _____

Date: _____

Unit 3 • Content Quiz

Part 1 True/False questions (25 points)

Decide if the following statements are true (T) or false (F).

_____ 1. Nitrogen is the most common gas in the atmosphere.

_____ 2. When you see stratus clouds, the weather is usually good and the sky is blue.

_____ 3. Polar climates are very cold and very dry.

_____ 4. Tornadoes form over warm ocean waters.

_____ 5. Another name for a hurricane is typhoon.

Part 2 Multiple choice questions (25 points)

Circle the best answer from the choices listed.

1. Which of the following is not a gas in the atmosphere?

   a. oxygen

   b. ozone

   c. carbon dioxide

   d. radium

2. Which of the following is not a layer of the atmosphere?

   a. stratosphere

   b. mesosphere

   c. unisphere

   d. exosphere

3. Which of the following is true about cumulus clouds?

   a. They are high-level clouds.

   b. They are sometimes called fog.

   c. You often see them right before a storm.

   d. They are fluffy and white.

4. What type of climate do the following sentences describe?

   This climate is neither very cold nor very hot. It has some rain but not a lot.

   a. tropical

   b. mild

   c. dry

   d. polar

5. Which country has the most tornadoes each year?

    a. The United States

    b. Canada

    c. China

    d. Ecuador

Part 3 Short answer questions (50 points)

Write a short answer to each of the following questions. In most cases no more than one or two sentences are required.

1. Give two reasons why people need the atmosphere.

2. Describe one type of cloud. Include details about what it looks like and what it can tell you about the weather.

3. What is climate?

4. Explain at least one similarity and one difference between a thunderstorm and a tornado.

5. Name the three main parts of a hurricane. Which part contains the most rain and the strongest winds?

Unit 4 • Content Quiz

Part 1 True/False questions (25 points)

Decide if the following statements are true (T) or false (F).

_____ 1. All organisms are made up of cells.

_____ 2. All plants grow from seeds.

_____ 3. Vertebrates are animals that have a backbone.

_____ 4. The heart controls everything we do.

_____ 5. Bones are heavy and strong.

Part 2 Multiple choice questions (25 points)

Circle the best answer from the choices listed.

1. Which of the following is not an organism?

    a. a person

    b. a dog

    c. a cloud

    d. a tree

2. Which of the following is not a symbiotic relationship?

    a. commensalism

    b. communication

    c. parasitism

    d. mutualism

3. The _____ is the largest part of the brain, and it controls most of our thinking and speaking.

    a. brain stem

    b. aorta

    c. cerebellum

    d. cerebrum

4. Which one of the following statements is true?

    a. Muscles protect the internal organs.

    b. When a muscle contracts, it gets longer.

    c. People can control all the muscles in their bodies.

    d. Muscles allow the body to move.

5. _____transports gases, water, and nutrients to all parts of the body.

   a. Blood

   b. The heart

   c. The left atrium

   d. Exercise

Part 3 Short answer questions (50 points)

Write a short answer to each of the following questions. In most cases no more than one or two sentences are required.

1. Explain the meaning of this sentence: Life on our planet is very diverse.

2. Give two reasons that many plant and animal species are losing their natural habitats.

3. Describe some of the physical characteristics and functions of the human brain.

4. What are two functions of bones?

5. What are blood vessels?

Photocopiable

Content Quiz Answer Keys

Unit 1

Part 1 True/False questions (25 points)

1. F   2. T   3. F   4. F   5. T

Part 2 Multiple choice questions (25 points)

1. b   2. d   3. c   4. b   5. a

Part 3 Short answer questions (50 points)

1. The response can include any of the following: the sun at the center of our solar system; the eight planets and Pluto; the contrast between terrestrial and gas giant planets; and the idea that planets orbit the sun and moons orbit planets.

2. The response should include one of the following examples (or similar examples) of how two or more systems are interconnected:
   - Humans are part of the biosphere, but they live on the lithosphere.
   - Humans are part of the biosphere, but they pollute the atmosphere when they fly on airplanes.
   - Lakes are part of the hydrosphere, but they provide the living things of the biosphere with the water they need.

3. The response should discuss one of the following rock types:
   - Igneous rock forms when magma rises up through Earth's crust and cools. Sometimes magma cools under the surface of Earth, and sometimes it erupts from a volcano as lava and cools on the surface.
   - Sedimentary rock forms when small pieces of rock break off and form a layer of sediment at the bottom of a river or ocean. Over time, more layers of sediment form on top of the first layer, and the weight from all the layers presses the sediment so tightly together that it eventually becomes solid sedimentary rock.
   - Metamorphic rock forms when the heat and pressure deep inside Earth change one type of rock into another.

4. Wegener's continental drift theory suggests that millions of years ago, Earth had just one giant continent, Pangaea. Over time, Pangaea broke apart, and the pieces drifted, or moved, to where the continents are today.

5. Positive effects of volcanoes include the formation of new mountains, new islands, and new land. Negative effects include the destruction of towns and cities, the death of many people, and dramatic and harmful weather changes.

Unit 2

Part 1 True/False questions (25 points)

1. F   2. F   3. T   4. T   5. F

Part 2 Multiple choice questions (25 points)

1. b   2. d   3. a   4. c   5. d

Part 3 Short answer questions (50 points)

1. We do not run out of water because nature keeps recycling water in a process called the water cycle.

2. The response should state one similarity and one difference between a river and an ocean. Similarities can include the following: They are both surface water features. They are both part of the water cycle on Earth. They both provide food and recreation for people. Differences can include the following: Rivers contain freshwater, but oceans contain salt water. Rivers are narrow, but oceans are wide. Oceans are bigger than rivers. Oceans have waves and currents, but rivers do not.

3. A glacier starts to form when snow falls and builds up layers that press down on each other until they become ice. The thick layers of ice become a glacier when they become so heavy that they begin to slide over the ground.

4. Near the equator, the heat of the sun causes a lot of ocean water to evaporate, and it leaves the salt behind. In addition, it does not rain much, so there is not a lot of freshwater to dilute, or weaken, the salty water.

5. A tsunami is a giant wave that forms when there is an underwater earthquake or volcanic eruption. When these fast, powerful waves reach land, they rise up high in the air and crash down, causing damage and killing people.

Unit 3

Part 1 True/False questions (25 points)

1. T   2. F   3. T   4. F   5. T

Part 2 Multiple choice questions (25 points)

1. d   2. c   3. d   4. b   5. a

Part 3 Short answer questions (50 points)

1. The response should include two of the following reasons: We need the oxygen (or breathable air) to keep us alive. The nitrogen in the air is necessary for the plants that we grow for food. The atmosphere acts like a shield and protects us from objects that fall from space. The ozone in the air protects us from the harmful rays of the sun.

2. The response should discuss one of the following types of clouds:
   - Cumulus clouds are fluffy, white, low-level clouds. When you see cumulus clouds, the weather is usually good, and the sky is blue.
   - Cirrus clouds are thin, wispy, white clouds high in the sky. When you see cirrus clouds, it usually means that stormy weather is coming.
   - Stratus clouds look like thick, gray, shapeless blankets that cover most of the sky. When you see these low-level clouds, you might soon see rain.

3. Climate is the average weather conditions of an area over a long period of time (at least 30 years). It includes the average temperature and the average amount of precipitation.

4. The response should state one similarity and one difference. Similarities can include the following: Both can cause damage and death. Both occur all over the world. Both are usually short storms. Differences can include the following: Thunderstorms are usually harmless, but tornadoes are usually dangerous. Flooding is the most dangerous part of thunderstorms, but powerful winds are the biggest danger in a tornado.

5. The three main parts of a hurricane are the eye, the eyewall, and the spiral rain bands. The eyewall contains the most rain and the strongest winds.

Unit 4

Part 1 True/False questions (25 points)

1. T   2. F   3. T   4. F   5. F

Part 2 Multiple choice questions (25 points)

1. c   2. b   3. d   4. d   5. a

Part 3 Short answer questions (50 points)

1. The sentence means that there are many different species of plants and animals on Earth. They are all different shapes and sizes, and they live in a wide variety of places.

2. The response should include two of the following reasons: natural disasters; pollution; human activities, such as deforestation and the development of land; and environmental changes, such as global warming.

3. The response should include some of the following: The human brain is quite small. An average brain is the size of two fists and weighs about 1.4 kilograms. Some people say it looks like a soft, pink, wrinkled rock. Others say it looks like a sponge. The brain has three main parts: the cerebrum, the cerebellum, and the brain stem. The human brain allows people to think, speak, see, hear, taste, smell, feel, move, breathe, dream, remember, use language, make music, create art, and develop complex tools and technologies.

4. One purpose of bones is to protect the internal organs (the skull bones protect the brain, the ribs protect the heart, and the backbone protects the spinal cord). Another function of bones is to help support the body (like the femur, or thighbone, which supports the weight of the body as we walk and run).

5. Blood vessels are small tubes that carry blood through the body.